ANTOINE
PREDOCK

ANTOINE

PREDOCK Architect

Compiled by Brad Collins and Juliette Robbins

RIZZOLI
NEW YORK

First published in the United States of America in 1994 by
Rizzoli International Publications, Inc.
300 Park Avenue South, New York, New York 10010

Library of Congress Cataloging-in-Publication Data
Predock, Antoine.
Antoine Predock, architect/introduction by Antoine Predock:
Compiled by Brad Collins and Juliette Robbins.
p. cm.
Includes bibliographical references.
ISBN 0-8478-1697-4 (hardcover) – ISBN 0-8478-1698-2 (paperback)
1. Predock, Antoine – Catalogs.
I. Collins, Brad.
II. Robbins, Juliette.
III. Title.
NA737.P67A4 1994   94-33118
720'.92–dc20   CIP

Cover Image: American Heritage Center, Laramie, Wyoming
Photograph © Timothy Hursley

Front Inset: Nelson Fine Arts Center, Tempe, Arizona
Photograph © Timothy Hursley

Back Flap: Nelson Fine Arts Center, Tempe, Arizona
Photograph © Timothy Hursley

Designed and Composed by
    Group **C** Inc
    BC, LH, DK, JDR, JLR

Printed and bound in Hong Kong

for Hadrian and Jason

CONTENTS

NOTES

New Mexico has formed my experience in an all pervasive sense. I don't think of New Mexico as a region. I think of it as a force that has entered my system, a force that is composed of many things. Here, one is aimed toward the sky and at the same time remains rooted in the earth with a geological and cultural past. The lessons I've learned here about responding to the forces of a place can be implemented anywhere. I don't have to invent a new methodology for new contexts. It is as if New Mexico has already prepared me.

In Australian Aboriginal dream time, song lines traverse the land and describe the geography in a way that is totally rational and yet mystically poetic. Similarly, the elemental power of this place is inescapable. In the making of architecture here, one has no choice but to deal with the basics of wind direction, movement of the sun, and other natural phenomena. But there is always another admixture that I call, in a blanket way, content. It's an aura that one cannot invoke in one's work. It's there or it isn't. It is like the idea of *duende* in a Flamenco performance; *duende* means "elf" in Spanish, but it also means a manifestation of spirit in a performance, rendering it transcendental and timeless.

Crucial to the spirit in my work is the enigmatic quality of the desert. You think you've got it, you think you understand; then you turn over a rock or crawl under a larger rock and you discover other worlds, other realms within. In a highway roadcut, for example, a sectional diagram of the earth is revealed through man's intervention. At the bottom of a roadcut in the Southwest is pre-Cambrian granite, overlaid by limestone. In geologic time, other sedimentary strata like sandstone and ocean bottom fossils begin to turn up – brachiopods, chrinoid stems. Then you begin to see cultural

9

One of my favorite journeys is Robert Smithson's trek through the desert where he rearranges the desert in his own way, aligning stones in different

artifacts, in relative scale, just a fraction of an inch compared to the miles of depth of the geologic datum. Prehistoric traces become visible, and then the successive cultural strata. In this section, after Anasazi traces, are later cultures: the arrival of the conquistadors, 1930s hubcaps, beer cans, McDonald's wrappers, and the residue of future technologies or whatever else you might imagine out there – the completion of the roadcut involves a sense of time beyond, that which is unknown but almost palpable here in the Southwest. The roadcut is a diagram of an investigative process for the making of architecture.

In the Southwest, I always think of the fundamental connection between the earth and sky through the mute, blank adobe walls that you find here. This has influenced me enormously. There is such a completeness in adobe architecture; the wall acts as a bridge between earth and sky. It is of the earth, an extension of the earth aspiring toward the sky, and any sort of decorative addition, a cornice or a stringcourse, would feel secondary and half-hearted compared to the power of the wall itself.

In my work, the connection to the sky is always there. I talk about going into the sky and into the earth simultaneously, and I often mean that quite literally. The Turtle Creek House (pp. 180–197) has a ramp that aims toward the sky, establishing a trajectory that one follows on ascent. My buildings in the desert are dug into the site, right into the ground.

When I was a student at Columbia University I became very involved in dance and with the body in space through the work of Jennifer Masley, Merce Cunningham, Yvonne Ranier and, later, Anna Halprin. This influenced my work profoundly. I think of my buildings as processional events, as choreographic events; they are an accumulation of vantage points both perceptual and experiential.

At the Mandell Weiss Forum (pp. 130–147) one comes through a eucalyptus grove and there, in a clearing, out of the blue, stands a two-hundred-and-seventy-foot-long mirror. One is suddenly part of the procession of arrival, just as when entering a theater, there is a sense of expectation, a murmur in the crowd, a building of tension that has to do with the arrival of the audience and the anticipated arrival of the performers. It is a ritual – the encounter with this giant mirror, the collective straightening of the tie, and the passage through the looking glass to what lies beyond.

The Nelson Fine Arts Center (pp. 42–79) seems initially to be a single event, but it is actually a series of vantage points, places that go into the ground and into the sky, episodically organized around a processional route that is open-ended. Visitors can create their own paths to unexpected destinations that provide respite from the sun and are, simultaneously, a celebration of the sun. The building offers an array of sensory possibilities throughout the day and the night. Its nocturnal life is very different from its sun-drenched daytime life.

The processional ordering of the building, as with many of my buildings, can be likened to a freeway interchange. Visitors can pass straight through the building to go to class or to the theater, or they can drop away or climb up, exploring an area off the main route. All the courtyards and *placitas* are usable for theatrical events, with the distinction between audience and performer always confused. The building, on many levels, is about dissolving boundaries and expectations.

Sometimes a building's connection to place starts with a silhouette, the notion of silhouette. When we come west for the first time and try to get our bearings, there is a daunting confrontation – the limit-less landscape, a limitless sky, distant mountain ranges iconically marking the land. I understand the tendency toward monumentality, ersatz monumentality, when confronted by the onslaught of this

unexpected way stations, sometimes there is a trailhead, sometimes a trail end. Sometimes the sky is the trail end. In my work the sky is both

infinite space. How does one go up against a mountain range? One option is to make something comfortable like a classical pediment, the impulse that has traditionally been followed in false-front western towns. Another option, one that I have chosen, is to make buildings that suggest an analogous landscape.

The pyramidal library in the Fuller House (pp. 30–41) is really more about a mountain, like those silhouetted on the horizon behind the house, than it is about the pyramid. The American Heritage Center in Wyoming (pp. 198–215), among other things, is an abstraction of land forms in the area, the mountain and the mesa. The building introduces an "archival mountain" into the landscape, with a village, the art museum, at its base. The project also manifests cultural readings, a sense of rendezvous, that timeless quality of meeting on an open landscape that we can trace from Native Americans to French trappers to Anglo settlers. It is about the desire to mark the land iconically, to beckon across great spaces, and deliver on that invitation. It is about connections and isolation.

From within, the building establishes a series of vantage points that track the sun and isolate views of particular moments, especially views west toward Medicine Bow Peak that are captured in the apertures of the west stairway. Other fragments of views almost deny the panoramic impulse of seizing the wide-angle view of the West so that one can encounter that very personally. I refer to the openings as apertures and not windows because an aperture has an obligation that a window doesn't have. It is not just about views and light, it is about magic, capturing, harnessing the power of a distant mark on the land and reinforcing that connection.

The notions of invitation and connection are critical and occur on many levels. They occur from a plane flying into the Laramie airport or from a car coming down the Interstate from Cheyenne. Approached in that way, the building also suggests an ancient helmet erupting from the prairie. Its ambiguous evolving copper patina, inspired by the sculpture of Constance De Jong, reinforces that image.

But the work isn't intended merely to evoke an ancient source, a comfortable icon. The aspiration toward the making of a timeless architecture should also contain an aspiration toward social responsibility. La Luz Community (pp. 20–35), from 1967, demonstrates a reaffirmation of the large-scale use of adobe brick in the context of a project whose five-hundred-acre site plan was based on sustainability and protection of the ecosystem. The Beach Apartments, a seventy-four-unit "low rider," combined subsidized housing with middle-income rental units while reinforcing the Rio Grande Valley cross-cultural crossroads site. And through the years, various publicly funded cultural facilities that I have designed have followed the same principles. But the social and programmatic face value of a project must be sustained by an underlying, less tangible, intention.

Architecture is a fascinating journey toward the unexpected. It is a ride, a physical ride and an intellectual ride. I like to think about machines and technology in relation to landscape and architecture. The idea of a machine in the landscape confirms a kind of closure for me, a technological, experiential, landscape-driven, artistic closure. Riding an extraordinary machine like a 1951 Vincent Black Shadow motorcycle across the desert, I am physically taking part in the completion of a circle. However, that sort of understanding, the relationship of technology to this place, has to be informed by the admission that we're really interlopers here. The fact that I'm here involves a mediating layer. I'm this gringo from nowhere, with Chaco Canyon culture out there dating from the eleventh century,

13

with even earlier vestiges around the West, and full-blooded descendants of those cultures around me. This, for me as an "American," carries a certain burden.

There is also the burden of stylistic distractions which are omnipresent and compelling in the world of architecture. Theories derived from other disciplines have broken new ground and opened channels of understanding. Everything influences my work. Anything that comes along is potentially of great interest to me; it can be something theoretically based or it can be the most ephemeral topical information. Making architecture is process-intensive work. It is not about a style or some master vision that I deploy each time. It's not that. When anything becomes an "ism" it accrues a shelf life, like a can of dog food. "Isms" are applied after the fact.

When I am working on projects with my team – and it is important to underscore the collaborative component in my work – we remind ourselves that we are involved in a timeless encounter with another place, not just a little piece of land. All of the readings that have accumulated and been assimilated there, that are imagined there, that may happen there in the future – all of these collapse in time and become the raw material with which we interact. We are not merely trying to record or express a particular epoch.

One could draw a line in the sand. On one side is a positive belief in the future, a future charged with potential. On the other side are, at an extreme, scary permutations of cyberspace – where Mary Poppins meets William Gibson. Both sides are okay, and it's possible to straddle the line. You don't have to be on one side or the other. There are exemplary realms that architecture can yield glimpses into, realms that are optimistic. Conversely, there is nihilism – making a thing of the chaos, making a thing of the mediation of our world – literal extrapolations. But to say casually, as some individuals

14

do, "I am going to be chaotic because of chaos theory," or "I'm going to be a deconstructivist architect because French post-structuralist literary critics talk about deconstruction," is highly suspect. There are a lot of disciplines to visit, a lot of stops to make, a lot of choices. But the choices made need to come from the spirit and from an understanding of the actual world around us, both in terms of the present and the past. So if it is possible, by living in New Mexico, to get back to some of the original visceral connections of certain experiences, in juxtaposition to the mediated realm that is immediately out there, that's a good position.

It encourages the making of something, the making of an object, where the making has a quality of innocence, where the gestural aspect of, say, making a clay model has an affinity with one's handwriting – with the presumed innocence of one's signature. That signature is part of the physiology of making something. In my case, whether it is a painting or a clay model or a collage, it becomes the beginning, the source for the project. Rather than being a highly rational methodology, my process remains connected to spirit through the body and to the personal space that the body defines. The trick is getting through the thicket of what Kahn called "the measurable" in the making of a building, to come out the other side with the original content, the original aura intact, for the built work to express that initial physical and spiritual impulse.

during the course of the journey, made visible from the contact of the building with the landscape, from the decisions about which trail to follow.

RIO GRANDE

Rio Grande Nature Center   Albuquerque, New Mexico

In the American wild West, the usurpation of nature has become a given, making this assemblage of a large area of wildfowl habitat within the Albuquerque city limits remarkable.

This site, on a major migratory flyway, is a 160-acre center for wild birds—sandhill cranes, snow geese, even an occasional endangered whooping crane.

16

The city acquired this land
from individual owners; the
state manages the facility.
Under this new arrangement,
farmers lease the land and
leave a certain percentage of
their crops as forage for
the birds.

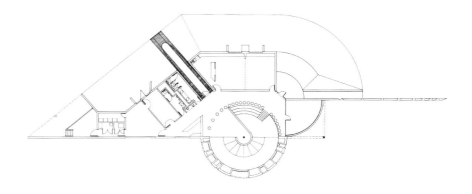

The building
can be thought of
as a permanent
viewing blind set
up with controlled
apertures offering
specific views of
the wildlife in its
20   natural habitat.

La **Luz** **La Luz Community   Albuquerque, New Mexico**

La Luz *means "the light"—the site is bathed in light.*

Sited on a semi-arid mesa above the west side of the Rio Grande bosque, this community of townhouses is a created landscape event: it retreats to the higher ground, optimizing

La Luz

the views east to the Sandia Mountains. From its vantage point, the community witnesses the changing

quality of light on the mountain face—from the black mountain rimmed in white at dawn to the roses, purples, oranges, and reds of sunset. Following the contours of the mesa,

24

the units step down the slope; this stepped section allows views toward the adjacent river landscape and distant peaks. But the primary motivation for the siting of

The approach to the damlike structure follows a circuitous path through a bosque and the great cottonwood trees of the valley. The entry is a truncated, corrugated-steel culvert through a bermed embankment.

The culvert recalls the water-management structures of the Rio Grande Valley. It invites visitors to pass through to the wetlands observatory, the light at the end of the tunnel. The culvert evokes a flow of water and is engaging for children.

25

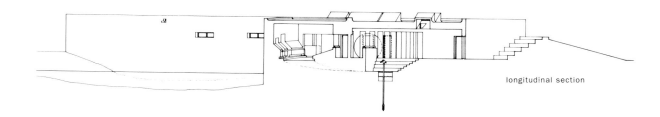

longitudinal section

New Mexico; that natural patterns should be recognized and reinforced. This site was ecologically vulnerable: it was critical that the floodplain areas—the habitat

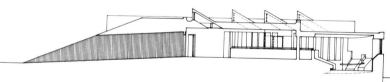

transverse section

The spiraling interior gallery space is surrounded by water-filled acrylic tubes, which have great thermal capacity. In winter, the sun enters through light monitors in the roof and its heat is absorbed by the tubes, adding to the energy efficiency of the building. But above all, the light-modulating tubes create a sense of an aquatic realm, especially in concert with the exterior pond visible through the view apertures.

Exhibits relating to both the wetlands and the wildlife follow a descending spiral ramp. At the hub of the spiral, a platform acts as an observatory, with views sweeping out across the pond and the Rio Grande Valley.

27

along the river, with its variety of wildlife (deer, coyote, fox, beaver, and migratory wildfowl)—be preserved. Though regulations would have allowed us to build in that zone,

The interior spiral ramp connects to ground level, where a galvanized-steel door leads to the natural preserve. An exterior courtyard serves as the trail head for nature walks that range from a short tour of the bosque to a three-mile circuit along the river's edge. In this manner, the exhibits extend outside the confines of the building. Visitors, as they head toward the preserve, are initially denied views of the wetlands. Then view apertures pierce the raw concrete exterior wall. They are different sizes and heights: tall adult, small adult, child, and wheelchair. These apertures underline the choice that must be made at the end of the wall: to return to the parking area through the cottonwood trees or to explore a nature trail.

the vulnerable areas of the site were kept at a distance from the community, and most open space remains protected by covenant. In contrast to the glass walls aiming

east toward the mountains and the city, the project presents a defensive posture toward the west—blank walls shield courtyards

FULLER

Fuller House   **Scottsdale, Arizona**

from low summer-sun angles and dust-laden spring winds. The courtyards themselves offer shelter from winter winds while acting as receptors that trap solar radiation.

31

The material is adobe, made on the site from excavated material, but no overt stylistic reference is made to southwestern adobe architecture. Glass is recessed beneath concrete

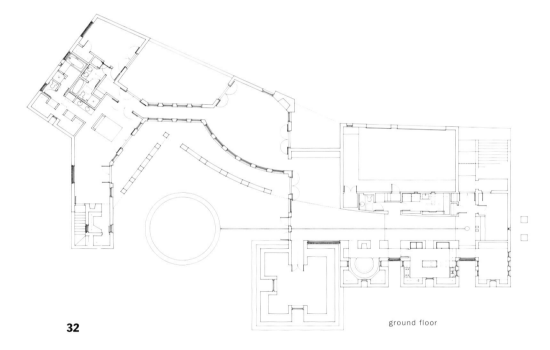

ground floor

32

This project links east and west with a sunrise terrace and a sunset tower. A source of water is contained in the space between. Daily living patterns shift from morning to evening: morning areas are to the east, and evening spaces, with vantage points for viewing the sunset, to the west.

fascias. The massive adobe walls serve as both heat reservoirs and acoustical barriers.

The exterior walls are

earth-colored stuccoed adobe with sand-blasted concrete lintels spanning openings. Some of the walls are stuccoed white to bounce light into a patio or room. Mountain views

La Luz

are visible from each of the homes in this community.

Boulders tumble into
the courtyard, suggesting
a dance, or the poetic
tension between land-
scape and architecture:
whether the landscape
will subsume the building,
as at Angkor Wat or
Chaco Canyon. That
tension is frozen here.

35

Inside, water issues from a black granite monolith and runs through a channel parallel to the east-west axis of the house. The water's path culminates in a quiet pool in the courtyard. The pool recalls a lake in a valley of boulders. A "crossfire" of water marks the entry, connecting visually with the black channel inside.

The house is axially positioned in relation to the east-west travel of the sun. Winter sun penetration is maximized and low summer sun angles are excluded. Trellises filter light across the sandstone floors.

39

Landshark **Landshark Lifeguard Tower** **Los Angeles, California**

Landshark

The Landshark is a tapered blade rising out of the sand.

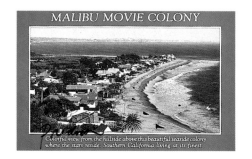

MALIBU MOVIE COLONY

Colorful view from the hillside above this beautiful seaside colony where the stars reside. Southern California living at its finest.

Constructed of carbon-fiber tubing.

The house is set deeply into the earth to provide thermal stability. Its views skim across the surface of the desert. The higher vantage points, like the sunset tower, have views across the valley toward the nighttime lights of Phoenix, to the sunset in the west, and to the mountains in the east.

41

the substructure is revealed through black kevlar mesh.

The Landshark evokes the power and mystery of the ocean.

Nelson Fine Arts Center   Arizona State University, Tempe

The design of the arts center, containing a museum, theater, and theater arts and dance departments involved a special attitude toward the desert—much more than simply imposing the building program on the quasi-urban university site. The harsh and relentless desert presence in Arizona is often denied; the prevailing tendency (in terms of development and attitudes toward public architecture) is to convert the desert into an oasis, to tame the desert.

42

It is legend engaging technology.

It is a Bedouin tent transplanted from the Sahara—a black ephemera that washes up on

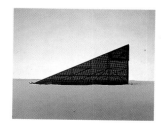

the shore. It is the myth of the ocean inverted: the Landshark is a beacon, an icon of protection.

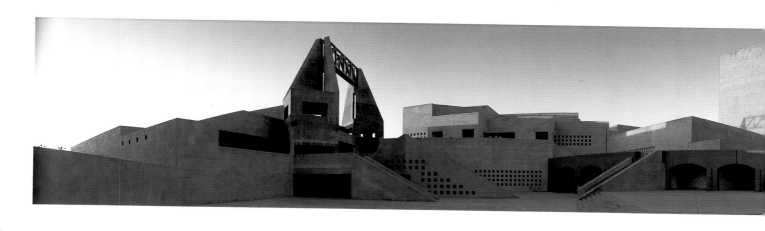

I did not want to deny
the power of the place or its
physical and mental assault.
It was important to face the
desert head on.

Ship of the Desert

Ship of the Desert   Nevada

ground floor

second floor

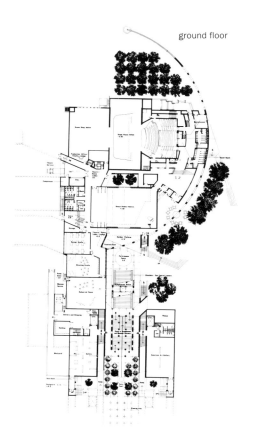

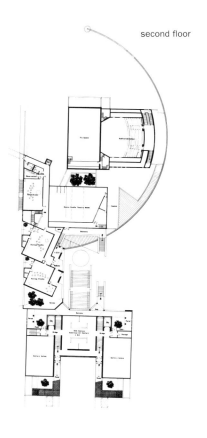

The desert is defined by the blazing sun and the need to find shelter from it. The arts center acknowledges this duality by linking earth and sky. The main entrance descends into the earth in search of coolness and psychological distance from the fierce sun above.

A new community has been planned where the fringes of the Great Basin overlap the edge of the Mojave Desert. "Colonization" will transform the desert landscape

and climate. What is now ragged brush and cactus will become an entire new town with a stark midday view of creosote bush and endless blue sky, with dramatic

Ship of the Desert

sunrises and sunsets highlighting the strata of the fault blocks and sandstone outcroppings of the nearby mountains. The information center and administrative office

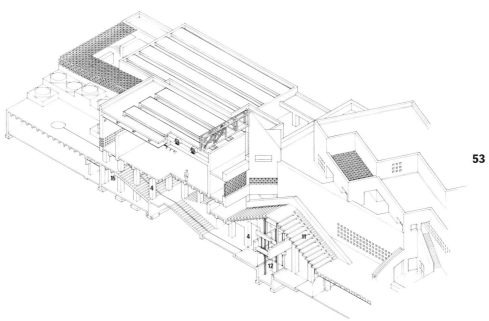

f Ship of the Desert houses a theater/meeting room, an exhibit area, and staff and public spaces. It is a sail, a tent that flutters in the breeze; its stone promenade deck is

Ship of the Desert

illuminated by fire. It serves as a visual focus and creates a desert preserve and gateway facility. Above entry level the building becomes increasingly ceremonial and

museum ground floor

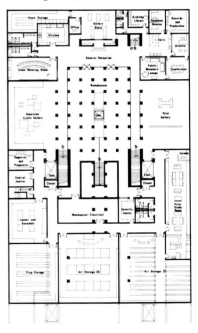

Gaps in the bleacher-like rooftop seating allow hot air to exit. Inside the subterranean courtyard, water evaporates to cool the air. These details work in tandem with the protective qualities of the earth.

less earthbound. From the reception desk visitors are directed upward into the red sandstone wedge, where images of the future are juxtaposed against glimpses of the present

Ship of the Desert

landscape. Atop the wedge, and again from the observation platform at the peak of the sail, the full panorama of the desert is revealed. The teflon-coated fiberglass

The building defines a journey, a procession; it defines options and potentials rather than particular paths or itineraries. It is an open matrix of possibilities for engagement both vertically and horizontally. **57**

59

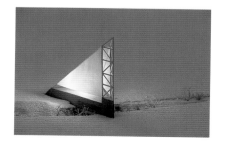

center initiates a journey. Settling into its substrate, lodged in the bottom of an arroyo, Ship of the Desert is returning home again.

61

United States Pavilion   World Expo '92, Seville, Spain

Art galleries extend the procession. They are anchored by exterior terraces for sculpture installations. These terraces are partly shaded by steel-plate trellises. The gallery sequence is open ended; visitors can use the sculpture terraces to explore inside and out, or they can proceed indoors to the large upper gallery, which has the highest ceilings and straddles the main entry.

63

The pavilion presents a vision of the American landscape recalling images in the song "America, the Beautiful." Its abstract, narrative topography is transformed

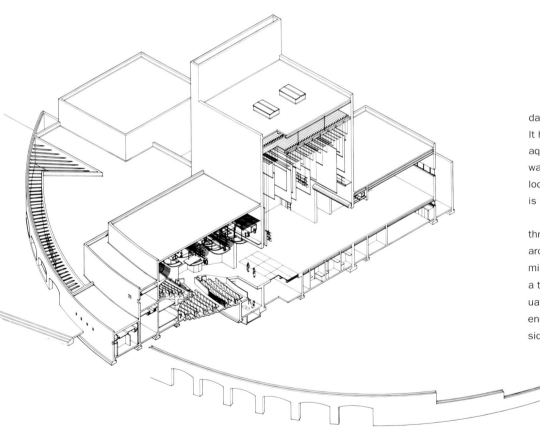

At the center is the dance studio/theater. It has a curving arcade-aqueduct that delivers water to three fountain locations, one of which is at the theater entry.

The theater is reached through the foreground arcade, which has aluminum louvers that form a trellis. The color graduates from light to dark, ending with purple-black sidewalls inside the theater.

as visitors explore it. The foreground is a growing wheat field—"amber waves of grain." At a scenic overlook visitors are greeted with a multilingual audio

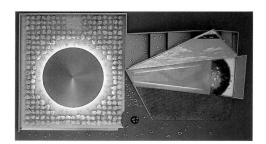

introduction. They progress into the shady "fruited plain" of apple trees where clearings provide space for outdoor performances and informal activities. The plain

surrounds the "purple mountain" theater—a hydraulically raised and lowered, conical, one thousand seat theater that houses the center piece film presentation.

When the conical mountain rises, bright white light and mist issue from the perimeter and the audience is admitted.

In addition to public areas, the building has intimate "inner sanctum" spaces: the black box studio/dance lab below the dance performance space, the acting and directing studios, a children's drama studio, rehearsal rooms, graphic studios, and all of the backstage functions that support the proscenium theater—the Galvin Playhouse.

United States Pavilion

As the visitors mingle in the cooling mist, the theatrical presentation begins. Emerging from the theater at the threshold of "stone canyon," the audience

exits through a dark chamber filled with a cacophony of American sounds, which are gradually replaced by the sound of rushing water. Visitors then ascend between two

great walls of water—"sea to shining sea"—that filter light into the multilevel glazed gallery and exhibition spaces. These galleries flank the axis leading

The poetry of Garcia Lorca describes the desert dualities: *"sol y sombra."* This building acknowledges those aspects of the terrain, both spiritually and physically. Necessary respites from the sun are created by zones of lacy shade, like the patterns paloverde leaves cast on the desert floor. Spiky trellis elements that evoke cactuslike images help to cool spaces both cavernous and labyrinthine.

71

to "echo amphitheater," where on the horizon a lone buffalo grazes in tall grass. "Spacious skies" are projected onto scrims that filter light to upper-level

Another journey extends to the sky, via terraces and balconies, toward towers that define the west campus entry as a gateway.

There is both an ascent and a descent from the middle ground, where the theaters and the theater-arts spaces are located. These multiple journeys are possibilities that become trails as each visitor experiences the building.

73

exhibition spaces. Other images projected onto the scrims develop the evolving narrative of the pavilion, portraying the character of America's cities, technological

74

United States Pavilion

achievements, and collective spirit. The pavilion reveals the many essences of America.

The procession has to do with adventure. There is a sense of exploration, of making spatial choices. It is newly engaging each time visitors pass through the building, whether they are students cutting through the building to go to class or the public arriving for a theatrical event or museum visit.

79

Agadir Palm Bay Resort and Casino   Agadir, Morocco

ZUBER
Zuber House   Phoenix, Arizona

This house is on the south-facing slope of Mummy Mountain. From that vantage point is a sweeping view of the valley Phoenix occupies. The valley serves as foreground for the house.

Camelback Mountain appears as an island in the valley. Considering the two mountains as islands, I wanted to back the house into Mummy Mountain, to excavate the mountainside and anchor the house within it, to create a cavelike impression and to associate water with the house, water from deep within the mountain.

The first encounter with the site suggested that it needed to be "healed." The long dune line paralleling the Atlantic coast had been breached by wave action that

also threatened a dense stand of black eucalyptus trees. The strategy was to use the six-hundred-thousand-square-foot first phase of the project to plug the gap in the dunes.

It was important to capture the panoramic sweep of the valley. The house, in plan, forms a T. The vertical leg engages the mountain, while the horizontal arm offers panoramic views toward the valley.

The "mountain house" is deeply recessed. It is constructed of rough concrete block using a colored aggregate that recalls the color of the mountain face.

The "panoramic house" is a lighter color and projects out from the mountain house. Its stucco finish is the gray-green of the desert floor.

82

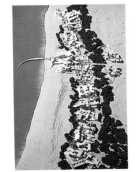

The arcing, scimitar-like curve of the breakwater is angled to resist the northwest course of the waves, protecting the dunes and a small harbor. A necklace of courtyards

linked by water, paralleling the shore but respecting the dune line, unifies the hotels and clubs. The sahat, *the central space, also follows an arcing configuration, which diagrams*

84

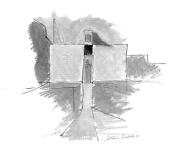

Agadir

the movement of the winter-solstice sun.

The exhibition halls are embedded in the earth. These act as

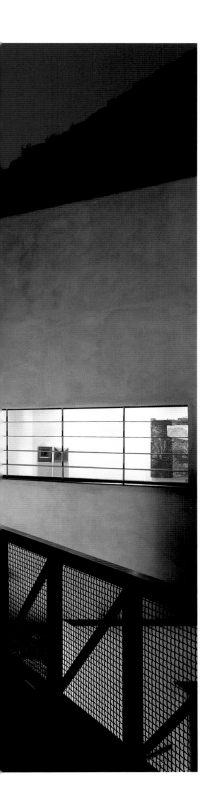

Connecting the mountain house and the panoramic house are two masonry towers. They are rotated to allow raking views of the city lights in the distance and the valley to the southeast. One tower sprouts a steel bridge that aims diagonally toward Scottsdale and aligns with local flight patterns.

The bridge is associated with both sky and night. The limestone paving blocks used inside the house flow outside to become the paving of the bridge. Inside, the joints between blocks are grouted with cement, but outside, on the bridge, they remain unfilled. Lit from below, these unfilled joints glow with possibility. It is a bridge that goes anywhere and nowhere.

85

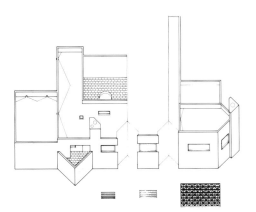

a substrate for the sahat *above, which connects the major elements of the program. The hotel, rising from the linked water courts and wrapping above the assembly spaces,*

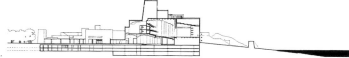

Agadir

allows direct views of the sea.

An egalitarian mix of tourists and locals reaches

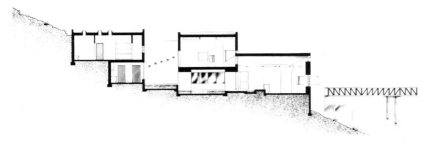

transverse section

...he beach through the eastern gateway, which parallels the arrival axis from the town of Agadir. This Mecca axis culminates in a ninety-foot-high titanium sundial

Agadir

whose winter solstice shadow tracks the arc of the sahat. The presence of the moon tower, Kamar, can be experienced in the reflection of flame on the titanium su

The house contains a sequence of water events. These vary from the contemplative to the active. Water descends in gentle steps from the mountain house, where the study-cave contains a silent pool. The water continues over a small cascade to a diagonally rotated pool and, finally, to a channel that leads into the entry space of the house. Each event illuminates different aspects of water.

89

The upper-level master suite, in the panoramic house, resembles a cockpit looking out across the valley toward Camelback Mountain. Long horizontal apertures frame views from the bed to the city lights. Water courts that descend under the master bedroom are open to the air, which is cooled as it moves over the water.

91

Las Vegas Library and Children's Museum   Las Vegas, Nevada

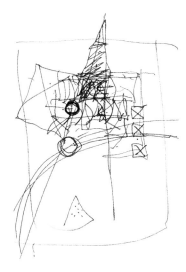

Las Vegas is a crossroads city. You have to get past the glitz to understand that Las Vegas has a history that begins with a palpable and visible geologic time. The surrounding mountain ranges expose layers of strata suggesting ancient upheaval. Over that is the layer of Native American occupation: the Paiute tribe. The next layer is that of the Spaniards.

There is a trail called the Spanish Trail that leads from Las Vegas into New Mexico. The most recent historic trail is the Mormon Trail, which links the west coast, via San Bernardino, to Salt Lake City, passing through what was to become Las Vegas.

I envisioned the Mediterranean theme proposed as all-inclusive, and I approached the vast literature relating to the Mediterranean as a point of departure.

Mediterranean Hotel

We researched the early cultures, Minoan in particular; we read Camus; we read Borges's House of Asterion, *Durrell's* Dark Labyrinth, *and Miller's* The Colossus

The trails converge at a natural spring in the northern part of Las Vegas. The crossroads is associated with the spring and its nearby meadows. (*Las Vegas*, in Spanish, means "the meadows.") An adobe-brick fort stands by the water at the crossroads. The site for the library and children's museum is adjacent to this fort and thus has a strong natural relationship to the earliest settlements. The library/museum building is also a cross-roads building. Its angular alignment receives oncoming visitors in ways that recall the convergence of trails. The sandstone wedge of the common administration area is an arrow, pointing north toward Sheep Mountain.

97

of Maroussi. *I wanted to synthesize all of these incredible impressions of the Mediterranean in a resort hotel; simultaneously, the stratigraphy of the Mediterranean itself informed*

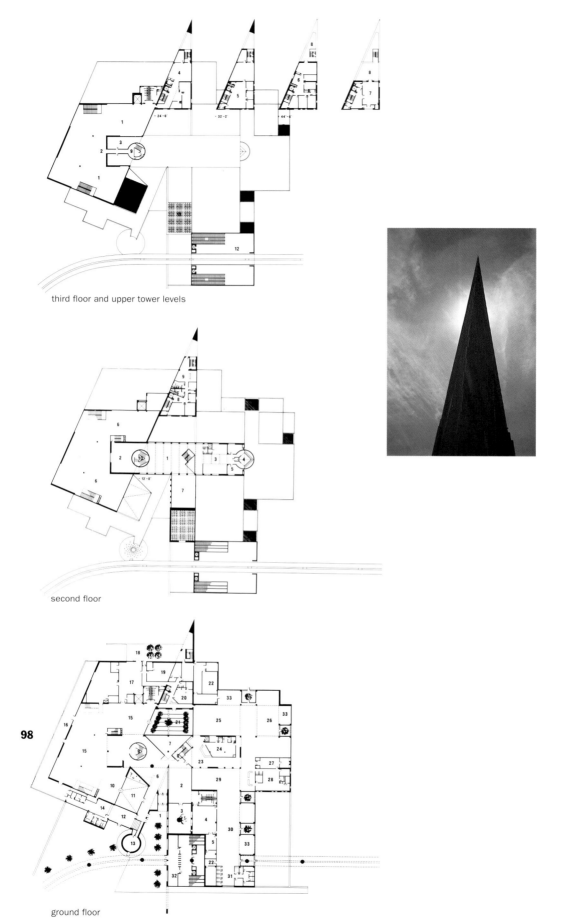

third floor and upper tower levels

second floor

98

ground floor

The pieces of the building diagram programmatic relationships as well as linkages between earth and sky. It is as though the building began as an orthogonal building until the "north arrow" wedge blasted through and sent the building askew. This skewing allows unrestricted circulation and creates a triangle of three courtyards within.

the spirit of the work. The labyrinthine courtyards and sensual gardens of the Mediterranean, as well as the white architecture of the region, seemed to work

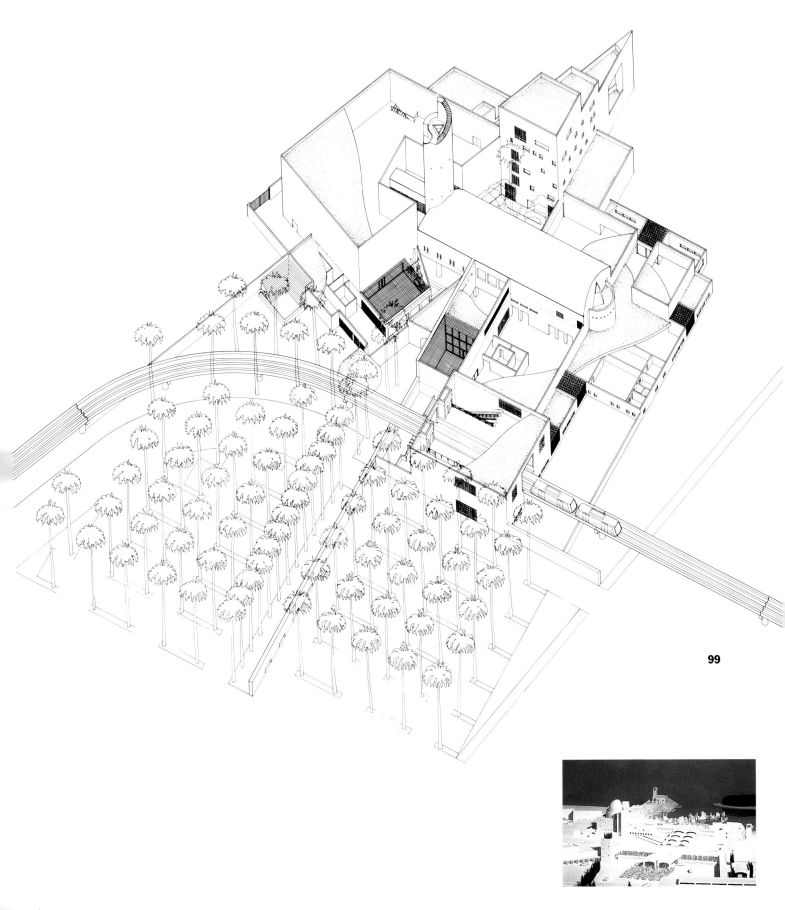

n Florida, not as literal extrapolations but as abstract readings. The site for the hotel, along the edge of a lake, was spectacular, and engagement with the water's edge was critical.

Upon arrival, the visitor is guided along the long north-south wall into the vaulted, tunnel-like entry. Water is discharged from apertures at the base of the wall. The presence of water is felt immediately; it is an elemental guide into the building, evoking the original presence of water on the site.

The water, which is recirculated, enters the building from the base of the wall and reappears in the central courtyard. The path of the water leads the visitor to this interior "oasis": a combination of palm and orange trees irrigated by the channels of the water system.

100

Mediterranean Hotel

One idea was to have an eruption issuing from the water to create a participatory pool for the visitors. In the end, the central "bay," where the water comes in

from the lake, became the swimming area for the hotel. Ambiguous architectural fragments scattered through the water suggest a timeless, non-specific culture.

102

Mediterranean Hotel

Departing from this central bay are guest rooms which embrace the water.

Other areas of guest rooms

The low-lying eastern portion of the building is the library. The large mass to the west houses the galleries. These sections of the building are connected by trellised courtyards.

The predominant material, other than sandstone, is stucco, the same white-hot color as the ground in Las Vegas.

103

surround linked courtyards; these also evoke the Mediterranean. Overall, I did not want the building to be high; I wanted it to be long and earthbound, a courtyard-oriented

At the far end of the barrel-vaulted children's library is the puppet theater/storytelling room. A triangular mirrored chamber is inset into its faceted glass apex to create a giant kaleidoscope that reflects a fractured vision of Las Vegas and the landscape beyond. An electronically operated partition covers the opening, sealing the space for puppet performances.

104

Mediterranean Hotel

building—a distillation of the Mediterranean readings with James Bond escapist overtones. Interpretation, both stylistic and environmental, was the important

The one-hundred-foot concrete science tower drills through the children's library and connects to the museum.

109

St. John the Divine   **South Transept   St. John the Divine, New York, New York**

The cone shaped "birthday party" room resembles a party hat punctured by irregular light apertures. These holes are located on a spiral defined by the Fibonacci series.

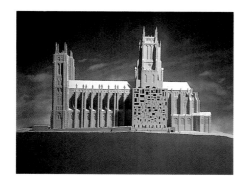

St. John the Divine

St. John the Divine, the Episcopal cathedral in Manhattan, reminded me of Chartres and the power instilled there but I felt the homage I would pay a true Gothic

uilding was not appropriate for this turn-of-the-century Gothic church. Instead I focused on the cathedral's "backstage"—the interstitial realm of the triforium galleries, the

St. John the Divine

spaces above the vaults, the stairs embedded in the buttresses — and began to appreciate the building as a mountain of stone. I decided that the south transept

would be another stone mountain and proposed that it be generated from an ordering system based on sacred Christian numbers—threes, sevens, twelves. The proportions of

114

the huge stone blocks, the spaces within and between them, and the negative spaces were derived from this Christian numerology. The cross section of the transept ha

ry heavy blocks at the bottom and smaller stones at the top. The facade—I actually referred to it as a "non-facade building"—was created by clipping off the system of numbers.

This house examines the relationship between land and water; it deals with the timeless aspect of Los Angeles—not the topical. Every possible intervention has been tried in L.A. in an attempt to transform it, to divert it away from its original landscape.

This house turns its back on the land, on the interventions. It focuses instead on the ocean by setting up a series of vantage points, some more accessible than others, that have to do only with the ocean and the imagined realms beyond.

116

Carving through the stone mountain is a ramp that escapes to the sky through the roof, taking as its axis the alignment of the summer-solstice sun at noon

he ramp's decreasing spiral defines a liturgical path with way stations—chapels—along its route. Also lodged in the stone mountain are thin sheets of marble arranged to

St. John the Divine

create an occupiable stained-glass window, one that can be encountered in three dimensions. The cathedral begins in the depths of th

roposed opening a capped spring under the church to form a baptistry below the transept. The program also asked that the transept be a "bioshelter," an organically based

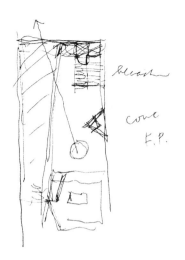

In the entry, the divergent lines of the granite "runway" reverse the perspective—space is collapsed and the ocean brought closer.

120

system that would recharge oxygen for the church, proposing an appropriate urban ecology.

At the end of the run-way is an eight-by-fourteen-foot aperture; its red, one-ton frame rotates on roller bearings. When open, the rush of the sea—the smell, the sound, the wind—invades the house in a remarkable way.

123

Substantial materials establish the foreground on the ocean side. The dark gray granite monolith is powerfully rooted but appears to dissolve behind a film of recirculated water. As the water meets the stone and merges visually with the ocean beyond— it manifests a critical original, primordial connection.

The armature that seizes and frames views from within the house is poured-in-place concrete. Different levels of the house align with openings in the armature. It is akin to bones along the shore—the skeleton of some giant creature.

Rosenthal House **Rosenthal House Manhattan Beach, California**

Immediately adjacent
to the red-glazed frame
is a three-by-seven-by-three-
foot subtraction from the
four-foot-thick armature.
One can stand in this
space and gaze through
a three-quarter-by-twelve-
inch deep fragment of
glass that was cast into
the concrete pour. Through
the glass is a kaleidoscopic
view of the ocean, the
sky, and the sand: very
dreamlike and very much
removed from the more
conventional views from
126   the other apertures.

The quality of light in the Los Angeles area is modified by the merging of sea and sky. The aqua cast of the house's glass, trim, and stucco reinforces th

ality. The upper level of the house, the sleeping lantern, glows delicately at night. Translucent floor-to-ceiling sliding glass panels can, in different combinations,

Rosenthal

change the color and ambience of the space within, creating different degrees of translucency from transparent to a dense, rich aqua. The manipulability

f that wall is in the spirit of the "toyness" of the house: it refers to the idea of transformation in toy design, the occupation of the client. In the rest of the house,

Going to the theater should
be a ritual, a ceremony.
The approach to this building
is a gift to the audience—
an experience heightened
by the eucalyptus grove that
defines the site.

In the center of the grove
was a clearing that became
the site for the building and
its 270-foot-long, 13-foot-high
mirrored entrance wall. The
mirror is detached from the
theater; it is a floating plane
poised against the eucalyptus
grove. When theatergoers
arrive they see their individual
and collective reflections in
this mirror, and they smell the
aromatic eucalyptus leaves.
The sounds of dry leaves
and gravel underfoot also
charge the arrival. There is a
true sense of expectation.

130

transformation is more ephemeral. Space is transformed by light. The mid-level studio is conventionally glazed, in contrast to the sleeping lantern. This

glass boundary allows an immediacy of interaction with the courtyard-terrace. The outer shell of the house embraces this terrace, binding it to the studio space.

MANDELL WEISS FORUM

Through the mirror is an exterior courtyard and then a switchback ramp. As theatergoers ascend, almost like voyeurs, they look back through the looking glass into "reality" and watch the arriving patrons. This experience precedes the real mission: to attend the theatrical event.

133

ffers focused, framed views to the ocean in the distance, out along the arms of the house, which form an X in plan. The lower level contains traditional residential

functions—bedrooms, bathrooms, living and dining spaces, all oriented to the courtyard and the vestigial 1950s kidney-shaped swimming pool which w

The mirror is particularly enigmatic at night. It can be either a one-way or a two-way system. Depending on the level of light, one sees through the mirror or is reflected in it. Sometimes at night a glowing light from behind the looking glass reveals furtive impressions of movement visible to approaching patrons. The mirrored wall becomes a threshold between the reality of the everyday and the dreamlike, mythic power of the theater.

135

art of the original house on the site. X now marks the spot.

Along the switchback ramp is a cantilevered black-steel landing, which aligns with the main entry road into the campus. This entry road cuts a notch through the eucalyptus grove, toward the Pacific Ocean.

From the approach to the building, this heavy balcony appears to be resting on nothing.

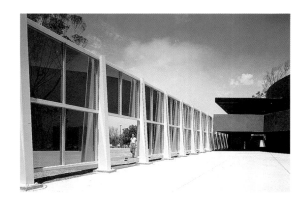

138

The ramp continues to an upper balcony, which is covered and protected by a cantilevered steel canopy. From here, one looks out over the mirror to the clearing below and to the Pacific in the distance. The top of the mirror has **140** become the balcony rail.

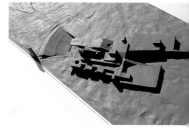

Clark County Government Center   **Las Vegas, Nevada**

ke a desert creature, this building burrows into the ground leaving behind a trail of detritus. A drive-in-movie-style amphitheater and a sandstone-clad canyon provide

142

critical public space at the north end and in the core of the building. Sequestered work spaces for the government employees wrap around the canyo

A metal-clad pylon aims north to the mountains as does the horizontally extending blade from which the movie screen drops. One journeys through the buildi

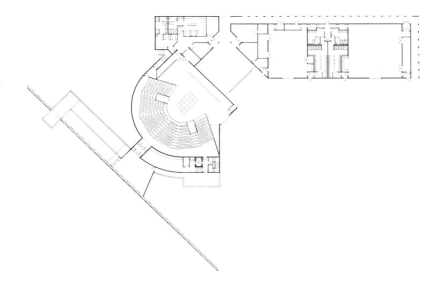

One finally enters the building on axis with the theater, which has a thrust stage and an amphitheater-like semicircular configuration. Suspended catwalks traverse it to serve both acoustic and lighting-access functions. Below the seats an actor's crossover allows entrances from multiple directions.

145

...cending to council chambers on roof terraces. Vine-covered trellises along with sunny, shady, and water-misted terraces extend from the chambers for events

The backstage functions are housed in the juncture between the theater and an arm of the building that contains rehearsal spaces. The courtyard is a major work venue for exterior stagecraft and also a gathering place for the people who use the building.

146

on summer evenings and in the cooler temperatures of spring and fall.

Inevitably, human settlement alters the landscape. Successive habitation has altered the Pomona Valley from the original dry swept earth of Rancho San Jose. Now the verdant Arabian horse ranch of W. K. Kellogg coexists with the technological, superscale freeway interchange.

The Cal Poly building is truly a gateway building, visible from the freeways, the local flight patterns, and across the entire Pomona Valley. The Kellogg ranch in the foreground provides a sense of a continuing agricultural presence — appropriate given the university's original agricultural emphasis.

148

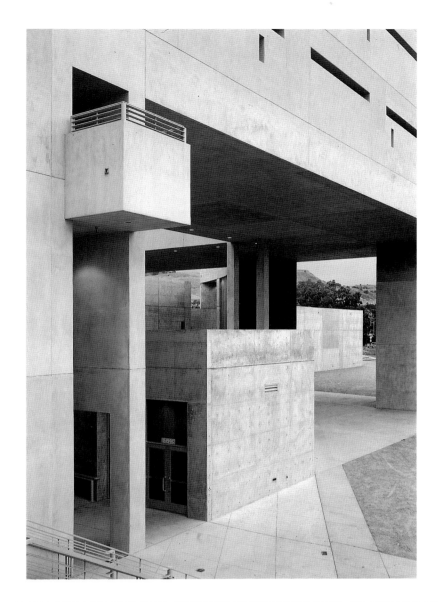

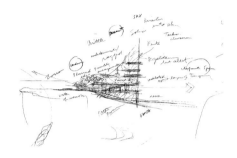

The building's silhouette delineates the different elements of the multifaceted program. The large tower houses a mixture of administrative, faculty, and student functions. The open-circulation classroom/laboratory functions as the organizational core for the remaining elements of the program: computer laboratories and classrooms.

151

Social Sciences and Humanities Building   University of California at Davis

The sharpest angle of the triangular plan points toward Mount Baldy in the San Gabriel Mountains. Upper-level terraces in the stone tower also direct views toward the range. The prow of the tower points in the direction of the Kellogg ranch. One corner of the triangular plan is clipped to nestle against a duck pond. These geometric adjustments anchor the CLA to the spirit of the Pomona Valley. The building becomes an abstract geologic form mirroring the surrounding landscape of basin, foothills, and mountains.

153

e University is in California's central valley, an area with a rich agricultural heritage. Watercourses carve through the surrounding fields. The building is an analogous

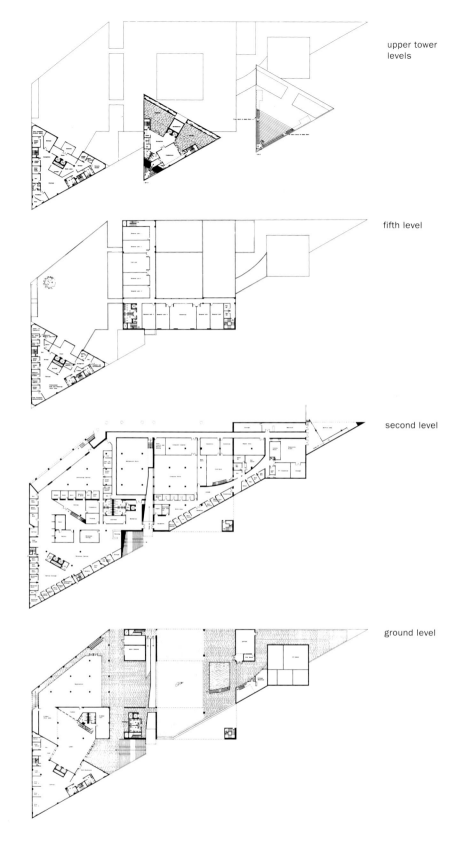

upper tower levels

fifth level

second level

ground level

The core classroom piece unravels around a central courtyard. In plan it begins as a square, becomes a U, an L, and finally an I. As it unwinds, views of Mount Baldy become increasingly dominant.

The building is locked into the land. Its base is at grade on the north and presents a one-story wall to the south. The level change opens a pedestrian path through to the main quadrangle of the campus.

154

Social Sciences and Humanities

composition: a curvilinear pedestrian route passes through orthogonal pieces. The low-lying blocks of the buildings are aligned with the campus and fie

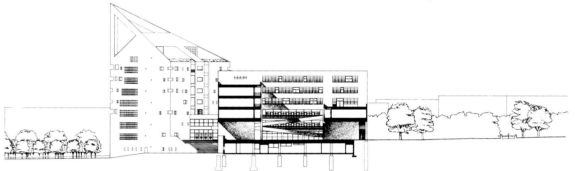

transverse section

155

longitudinal section

…ese blocks form a base for upthrust, sloping pieces that house offices and afford distant views. These pieces are clad in metal and at times seem to dissolve

The building is very permeable. It provides shortcuts to various parts of the campus, and the open zone under the raised classroom block serves as a meeting ground/gateway. From the courtyard, elements of the building's structure form a gigantic aperture opening to the Pomona Valley. It celebrates the school's connection to agriculture by focusing on the neighboring fields framed against the tawny hills of summer and the green hills of winter.

156

into the sky. A subterranean level, oriented to the pedestrian route above, is carved into the ground.

The departments in the building are given clear identities; their arrival points become departmental foci.

Visitors have a choice of routes to explore the campus. Each path establishes its own vantage points and gathering places, as well as clues about the building's overall structure. Although fragmented, CLA is not a collision of separate functions. It is instead an orchestration of stratified geometries that are evident as visitors pass through this gateway building.

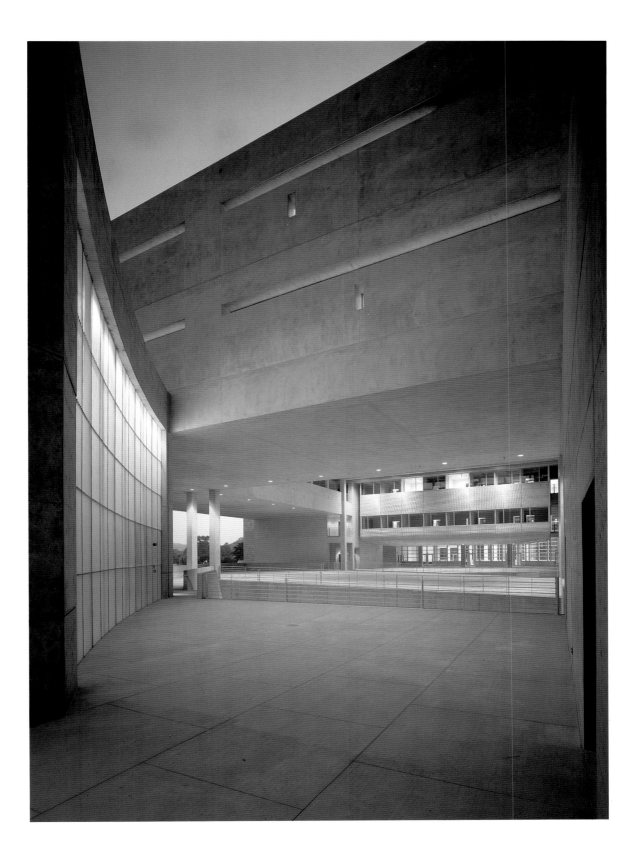

Thousand Oaks   Thousand Oaks Civic Arts Plaza   Thousand Oaks, California

Thousand Oaks is a "Godzilla-meets-Bambi" site. A sylvan meadow below the relentless Ventura Freeway evokes

162

the original landscape of this part of California—live oaks, tall meadow grasses, and a watercourse. The program includes a city hall for Thousand Oaks,

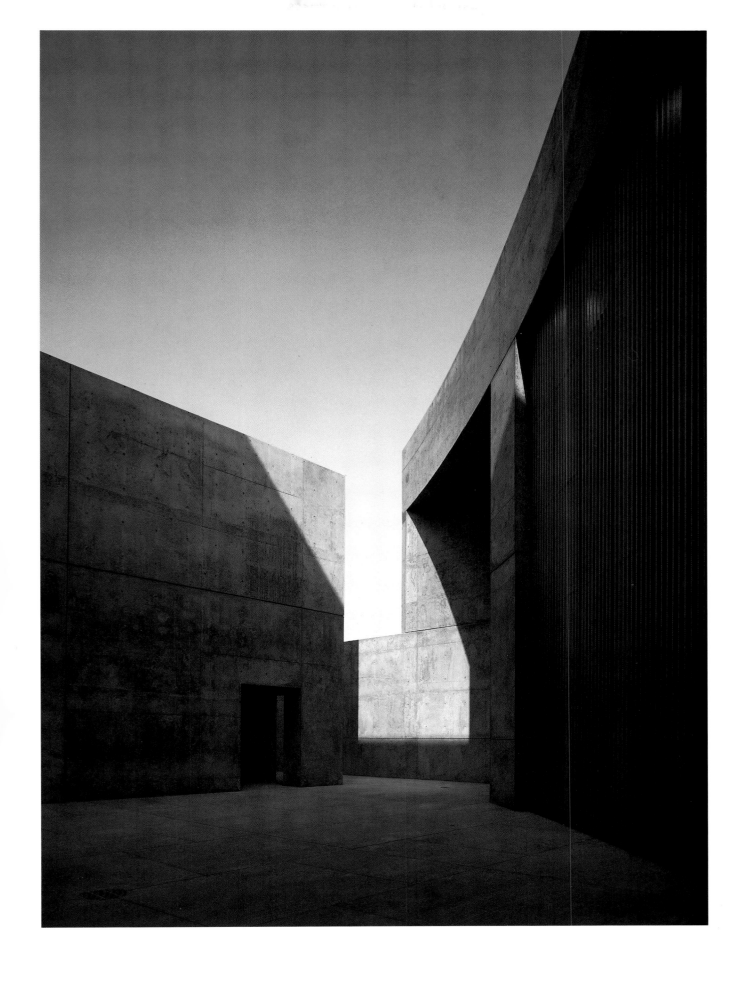

700-seat performance space, and a 400-seat council forum/theater. The theater pieces are positioned high on the site to block the freeway noise and to shelter

HOTEL SANTA FE

The notion of "theming" a building in France was dangerous. How literal could it be? How nostalgic should it be? Should it be there at all?

I wanted to project a vision of the West that surrounds me every day: a site of imagination. I thought the project should be like a Wim Wenders movie, like *Paris, Texas,* rather than have the sweetness and nostalgia of Santa Fe.

The hotel has a series of trails as an organizational system. Each trail departs from the horizontal commons building, which is under a drive-in movie screen. The trails create a matrix of events and a series of explorations that are particularly oriented to children. The exploration takes place in an architecture that is specific to France in terms of wind protection and sunny exposure.

164

the rest of the project, which intersects the meadow below. Workers in the city hall have both views and direct access to the meadow. The roofs of some of

...ministrative buildings double as terraces and can be used during performance intermissions.

The "trail of legends" begins with a volcano and four archetypal Western buildings, all containing guest rooms: a gold metallic block suggests the gold rush; a silver metallic block, coins or a bank; a raw concrete block, a jail; a red block, a bordello. A black-and-white building is deformed, set at an angle. It is a dissonant piece that recalls the black hat/white hat myths of the West— the tension between good and evil.

169

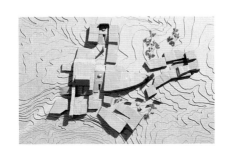

This "city for children" is organized around linked courtyards that suggest ageless ruins. One courtyard celebrates the dismantling of warplanes: the vertical tail

Ventana Vista

section of a B-52 bomber emerges from the ground like a shark fin. The fourth- and fifth-grade classrooms are organized around another courtyard whic

The "trail of monuments" contains dislodged fragments of buildings, some axially rotated. Here I was influenced by the reassembled landscapes of Road Runner and Krazy Kat cartoons. I wanted to include something of the way those cartoons used impossibly balancing rocks to signify the existence of a fantastic realm. Mostly, the "monuments" on this trail are improbable collages of elements that are analogous to accretions seen in the Southwest.

171

hrough the use of glass garage doors, can function as indoor/outdoor space; one of its walls is faced with slate to create an exterior chalkboard. The scale

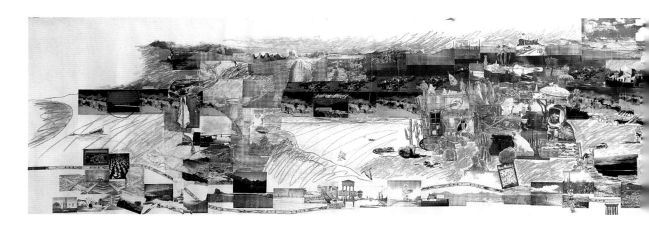

Ventana Vista

and character of the "neighborhoods" within this city vary with the age of the child. Kindergartners have a "turtle classroom"; windows are set eighteen inc

The "trail of artifacts" is organized along a path of broken aquamarine tiles inspired by a favorite turquoise-inlay belt buckle of mine. One artifact is a caged fake saguaro cactus: "saguaro in bondage."

Also along the trail is a collection of rusting cars. We found them in parts on North Fourth Street in Albuquerque: a 1932 Plymouth, a 1946 Chevy pickup, and a 1957 Ford Fairlane. They were packed into containers, shipped to Houston, and then to France, where they are embedded in a courtyard, suggesting the erosion and deterioration of the desert. Crashing into the top of one of the buildings at the end of the trail of artifacts is a fiberglass meteorite. These icons of the desert are just as interesting and ubiquitous as adobe ruins.

173

ve the floor so that children can gaze across the desert while lying down. The second and third graders have the "sorcerer's terrace"; it has a wall of apertures that align with

174

celestial events. In the "troll's lair," troll dolls are stapled to the ceiling by their feet and their fluorescent red and green hair hangs down. A reading space is bene

The "trail of water" issues from a mountain: the top of a building. At one point, the water dives down a one-hundred-foot course. When it reaches ground level, it is discharged in two directions.

One channel is geometrically ordered. Almost like an irrigation canal, it traverses a series of courtyards interrupted by a triangular fish pond and the dance of sprinklers. The other channel is naturalistic. The water travels along a rocky stream bed until it reaches a "geothermal event": steam issuing from the rocks.

anslucent dome, which acts as a desert kaleidoscope. Desert artifacts are lodged in the glazed orb. At a distance, this city for children nestles into the landforms of the site.

176

Ventana Vista

Emerging from its low-lying silhouette is a tent-like white canvas structure that recalls the nomadic occupation of the desert.

The "trail of infinite space" recalls the never-ending yellow line of the great American highway. The first element of the trail is the drive-in movie screen over the commons building, which is centered on an actual yellow line. Originally, the screen was a tabula rasa, an empty plane onto which one could project one's own fantasies, but eventually an image of Clint Eastwood was chosen. I was happy with this choice, not because he represents the West, but because in France he is revered as an artist.

The yellow line leads on; the hotel seems to converge around it, exaggerating the feeling of infinite space. At the end of the trail is a stainless-steel disk. Resembling a UFO, the disk slices into the ground, interrupting the trail.

TURTLE CREEK

Turtle Creek House   Dallas, Texas

This house, "theater of the trees," was a response to the client's passion for bird-watching. The site is at the convergence of two major continental flyways on the Turtle Creek watershed in Dallas.

The house is on a cul-de-sac off a busy street. One first encounters giant limestone ledges, which create a weighty and earthbound foreground: a dam of expectations. The ledges suggest a timeless relationship to the site, one that has geologic parallels to the Austin Chalk Formation, the spine that runs north-south through Dallas.

The ledges are filled with plants that birds love; this way, birds always greet visitors.

181

ampa Museum of Science and Industry

Tampa Museum of Science and Industry | Tampa, Florida

The site for the museum is adjacent to an active wetland full of wildlife. A causeway-like arm of the building

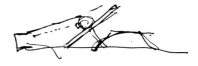

Tampa Museum

engages the immediate environment while simultaneously guiding the way from the busy northern entrance street to parking areas. Cars drive through

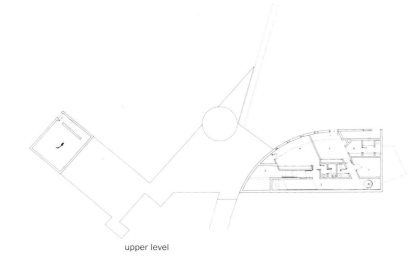

upper level

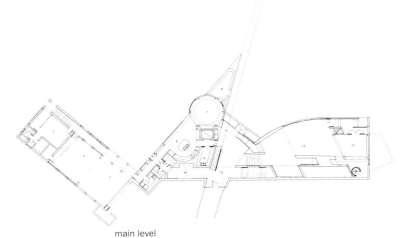

main level

Vantage points are poised throughout the house. They are directly related to characteristics of the local avian habitats.

A central "sky ramp" projects the fissure of the entry into the surrounding canopy of trees. This trajectory aims toward the sky. It touches the ground lightly, allowing the undergrowth to flow beneath it. Its predominantly tensile-steel composition resonates with the wind, like an instrument, blending with the music of the birds.

183

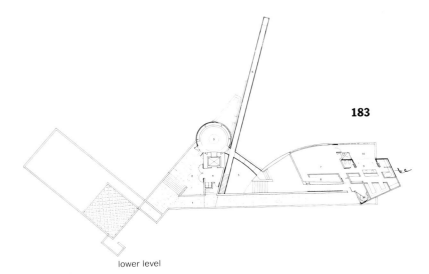

lower level

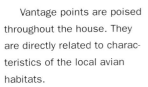

Tampa Museum

skin of the theater/sphere is of highly reflective stainless steel tinted to mirror the blue of the sky and the waters of Tampa Bay. The central gathering

185

ce in the observatory is surrounded by giant legs that contain light mechanisms. The geometry of the museum is a reorganization based on the grid of the existing

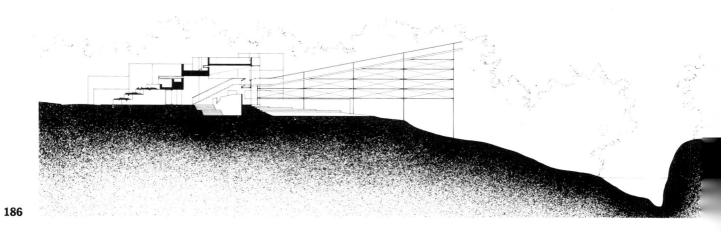

transverse section

pavilion-like science museum. One link between the two buildings is a causeway with tubes at the eye levels of children; these tubes project selected v

...wards events and objects at close range and on the horizon.

The entry fissure in the ledges is a channel that separates the house into north and south "houses." An interior black-steel bridge spans this entry hall. The hall's twenty-foot ceiling reveals the stratified tree canopy outside. The entry hall is also the point of departure to the various interior vantage points.

A gallery zone links the north and south houses. It parallels the limestone ledges and begins an interior trail that culminates in a network of roof terraces.

189

Arizona Museum of Science   Phoenix, Arizona

As an experiential journey, the building is based on the abstract integration of architect

The floating wall is an interior counterpart to an exterior stainless-steel mirror. It hovers above the floor plane of the living room, dissociating itself from the other walls. It is an object isolated by space and glass from the rest of the house.

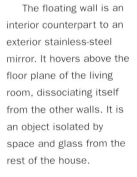

h the Arizona landscape. Visitors approach from the north; their first view of the building is a backlit silhouette with an aura of desert light. A metallic peak

These terraces and
walkways are oriented to
sunrise and sunset views
as well as to the Dallas
skyline. In addition, these
outdoor vantage points
are essential for watching
migratory wildfowl, both
resting and flying.

Arizona Museum

ascends above the museum galleries and the theater, aiming toward the stars. At the entry visitors descend into a subterranean lobby, which is washed

light from sunken courtyards. The shaded roofscape atop the galleries and planetarium, is a gathering place; trellised gardens and terraces form the roof

of the lobby; steps ascend above the arrival courtyard. Visitors journey from earth to sky, climbing in a path analogous to the nearby landscape of mount

The convex, floating, two-story stainless-steel mirror reflects the house yet also seems to absorb it. The distorted images of landscape, birds in motion, and sky confuse the stability of one's vantage point — like Plato's cave.

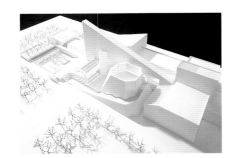

aks and canyons.

196

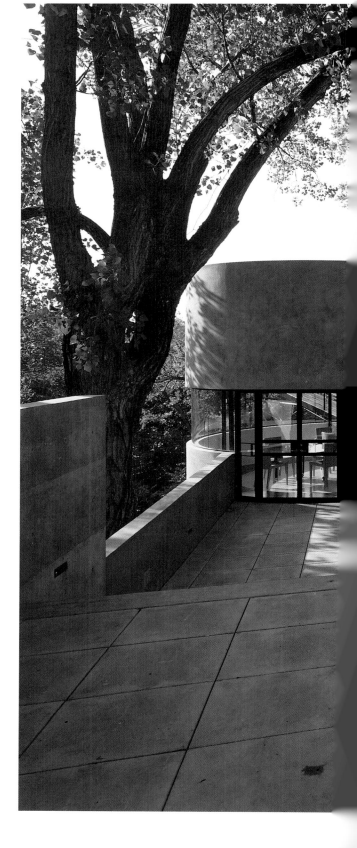

Baltimore Performing Arts Center   Baltimore, Maryland

The Performing Arts Center is an urban chandelier: it emanates crystal, celebratory light. T

andelier" is formed from a resin of crystalline glass. Internally, it seems as though the interstitial realm of the resin is occupiable, like a piece of amber.

American Heritage Center and Art Museum   University of Wyoming, Laramie

198

The theaters are fossils caught within this amber resin; projected into the facets of the chandelier from internal projection points are "media fossils": images t

Throughout Wyoming there is a sense of landscape in formation, of landscape in transition.

The appearance of this "archival" mountain can be thought of as parallel to the slow but certain geologic upheaval. **199**

ate to current performances and to Baltimore in general. The building is inexorably locked into the grid of this city. Baltimore's many grid lines weave a fabric when assembled,

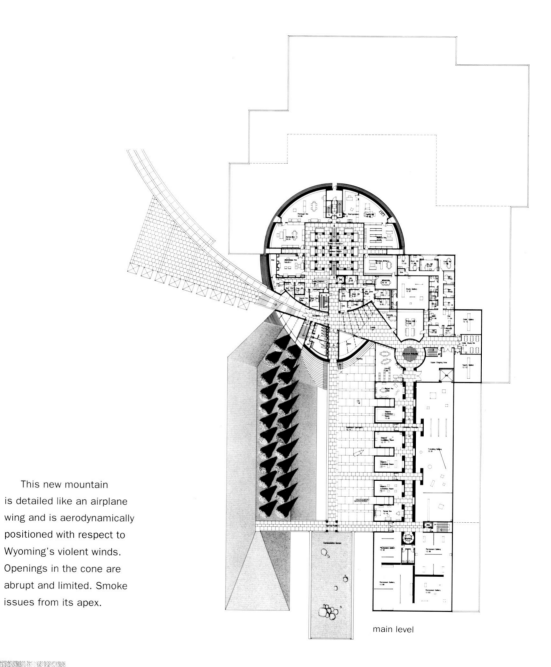

main level

This new mountain is detailed like an airplane wing and is aerodynamically positioned with respect to Wyoming's violent winds. Openings in the cone are abrupt and limited. Smoke issues from its apex.

200

Baltimore Performing Arts Center

and the plan of the center has been generated by connecting the dots in this fabric. The mass of the building and the facets within were then extruded from

ric-plan. The opaque fossil-like pieces—the 1800- and 650-seat theaters, the restaurant, and support spaces—erupt from the plan as limestone monoliths capped

The asymmetry of the mountain's stretched side guides visitors to a common ground between the American Heritage Center and University Art Museum, the two halves of the building. The entire structure is set on a mesa, a surrogate landform that absorbs archival and curatorial spaces below the public realm.

with metal. The resin of the chandelier blows around these pieces, cloaking lobbies and other public spaces in cascades of light.

The archival mountain axially linked to Medicine Bow peak to the west and Pilot's Knob to the east, and is also centered on axis with the nearby stadium. A web of site-specific references anchors the building to the campus and the landscape.

The art museum is reminiscent of a village at the foot of a mountain. It is poised on the mesa, with spruce trees on a bermed embankment establishing the foreground.

205

I call the building axis that links the two distant mountains the "rendezvous axis" because I see the building as a meeting place similar to those of Native Americans, French trappers, and early European settlers. Now it is a place of intellectual and social rendezvous.

AMERICAN HERITAGE CENTER

207

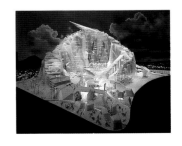

Atlantis Hotel and Casino   Las Vegas, Nevada

Atlantis

This project is about encountering architecture emerging and crystallizing both conceptually and physically. I interpret Plato's reference to Atlantis as ab

At the core of the mountain is a hearth with a timber armature that guides the flue up through the mountain to the sky. The floor levels wind around the hearth, each level rotating forty-five degrees, creating a spiraling ascent to the skylit center.

209

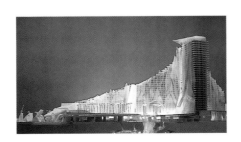

rrealism and time travel, not about history. This hotel is Atlantis; light emanates from a realm below, fragments of a subterranean culture erupt. The hotel proper

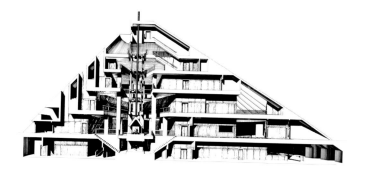

210

Atlantis

ascends from a fractured, tectonic plateau—established by the patterns of shattered glass—metamorphosing from stone and concrete into crystal. Th

oms of the hotel recall Superman's ice cave, the source of his energy. One of my ideas for the project was to host the television program "American Gladiators" there;

212

the whole face of the hotel could be a venue for the competition. A realm of water carves through the plateau at the base of the hotel. The watercours

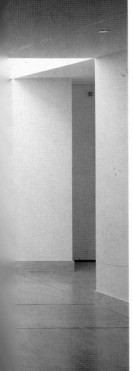

ads to a ramp; from there one can climb the building's nautilus spiral. A sixty-foot-deep vortex of salt water drills into the earth; divers can explore hidden grottoes

Atlantis

and a reef. The light that shimmers from the depths of the vortex implies a connection to a power source below. The view from the casino into the vorte

Cardinal points and representations of astronomical alignments are cut into the skin of the cone. In winter, light from the apertures beckons visitors, issuing an invitation across the barren prairie. As the black-patinated copper skin of the mountain weathers it will change and evolve. The building is in flux, mirroring its geologic situation.

215

s a further extension of Las Vegas' surrealism.

CHRONOLOGY

1978/80
Schwendi Restaurant
Taos Ski Valley
Taos, New Mexico
Burned in 1982

1970/72
First National Bank:
Sandia Plaza
Albuquerque, New Mexico
Altered

1967
Crib Cubed
Albuquerque, New Mexico

1978/82
Rio Grande Nature Center
Albuquerque, New Mexico
Pages 16–29

1967/68
Raven Townhouse
Albuquerque, New Mexico

1980
Tennis Ranch of Taos
Taos, New Mexico

1967/74
La Luz Community
Albuquerque, New Mexico
Pages 20–39

1971/73
Kaminsky House
Albuquerque, New Mexico

1975/76
Mountain House
Albuquerque, New Mexico

1980/82
United Blood Services
Albuquerque, New Mexico

1968
La Luz Play Structure
Albuquerque, New Mexico
Demolished

1973
The Citadel Apartments
Albuquerque, New Mexico

1977
Chant House
Albuquerque, New Mexico

1981
Santa Fe House
Santa Fe, New Mexico

1970/71
300 Twelfth Street
Predock House and Studio
Albuquerque, New Mexico

1974/76
Art Building
University of New Mexico
Albuquerque, New Mexico

1977/79
Albuquerque Museum
Albuquerque, New Mexico

1981/82
Chernush Addition
Arlington, Virginia

Maryland Center for the Performing Arts
Maryland Center for the Performing Arts   College Park, Maryland

The building, with its silvery metal roof, rises from a gentle slope, almost as if it were a geologic plane tilting upward

school, the performance art library, the dance department, and the theater arts department are ranged as a piedmont around the base of this limestone mountain,

1988/91
Mandell Weiss Forum
and La Jolla Playhouse
University of California
at San Diego
Pages 130–47

1988/91
Mediterranean Hotel
Walt Disney World,
Orlando, Florida
In association with
Flatlow Moore Bryan
Shaffer McCabe Architects
Pages 94–105
Project

1989/94
Thousand Oaks
Civic Arts Plaza
Thousand Oaks, California
In association with
Dworsky Associates
Pages 161–65

1987/94
Mesa Public Library
Los Alamos, New Mexico

1988/91
Venice House
Los Angeles, California
Pages 116–29

1988
Clarendon Baths
Ketchum, Idaho
Project

1989
Spectral Slug
(Play structure)
Des Moines Art Center,
Iowa

1989/96
School of Music
University of California
at Santa Cruz

1988
Estate
Mercer Island, Washington
Project

1989
United States Pavilion
World Expo '92,
Seville, Spain
Pages 62–72
Project

1990
Agadir Palm Bay
Resort and Casino
Agadir, Morocco
Pages 79–89
Project

1990/94
Social Sciences and
Humanities Building
University of California
at Davis
Pages 152–61

1988/91
Winandy House
Phoenix, Arizona

1988
Incense burner
Albuquerque, New Mexico

1988/92
Hotel Santa Fe
Euro-Disney,
Marne-la-Vallée, France
Pages 164–79
In association with
Fernier & Associés

1989/92
Institute of American
Indian Arts Museum
Santa Fe, New Mexico
In association with
Louis L. Weller Architects

1990/91
United States Olympic
Hall of Fame
Colorado Springs, Colorado
Project

1990/95
Tampa Museum
of Science and Industry
Tampa, Florida
In association with
Robbins, Bell & Kuehlem,
Architects
Pages 181–86

1988
Landshark
(Lifeguard tower)
Los Angeles, California
Pages 39–42

218 Project

which itself houses the concert hall. A public realm cuts through the base of the building, connecting to the lobby, a partially glazed canyon within the mo

1990/96
Arizona Museum of Science
Phoenix, Arizona
In association with
Cornoyer Hedrick
Pages 190–94

1991
Solana Office Building
Fort Worth, Texas
Project

1991
South Transept
St. John the Divine
New York, New York
Pages 109–21
Project

1992
Clark County
Government Center
Las Vegas, Nevada
Pages 138–44
Project

1992
Texas Rangers
Baseball Park
Arlington, Texas
Project

1993
House
Beverly, Massachusetts
Project

1993/94
Atlantis Hotel
and Casino
Las Vegas, Nevada
Pages 207–15
Project

1993/94
Baltimore Performing
Arts Center
Baltimore, Maryland
In association with Ayers
Saint Gross
Pages 196–202
Project

1993/94
Maryland Center
for the Performing Arts
College Park, Maryland
Pages 216–23
Project

1993/95
Center for Integrative
Studies Expansion
Stanford University
Palo Alto, California

1992/93
Bookstore and
Parking Structure
University of New Mexico,
Albuquerque
Project

1992/94
Ventana Vista
Elementary School
Tucson, Arizona
In association with
Burns and Wald-Hopkins
Architects, Inc.
Pages 168–76

1992/96
Student Affairs
and Administrative
Services Building
University of California
at Santa Barbara

1993/95
Hispanic Cultural Center
Albuquerque, New Mexico
In association with
Pedro Marquez
Architect AIA
Pages 223–32

1994/95
Butterfly Pavillion
Tampa, Florida
In association with
Robbins, Bell & Kuehlem,
Architects

1994/96
Spencer Theater for the
Performing Arts
Ruidoso, New Mexico

1994/97
Nano Technology Building
Rice University
Houston, Texas
In association with
Brooks/Collier

219

black box: a theater space spanned by catwalks with projection scrims hanging from the ceiling. It is rigged like a theater and is a performance venue unto itself.

SELECTED AWARDS

1993

Merit Award
AIA/Los Angeles Chapter
Design Awards Program
CLA Cal Poly

Award for
Excellence in Architecture
Western Mountain Region
AIA
CLA Cal Poly

Award for
Excellence in Architecture
Western Mountain Region
AIA
*Mandell Weiss Forum
and La Jolla Playhouse*

Honor Award
AIA/Southern Arizona
Chapter
*Ventana Vista
Elementary School*

Excellence for Energy
Efficient Design
Southern California Edison
CLA Cal Poly

Merit Award
AIA/Cabrillo Chapter
Rosenthal House

1994

Award of
Excellence for Design
*Architectural Record:
Record Houses
Turtle Creek House*

AIA National Concrete
Masonry Association Award
*American Heritage Center
and Art Museum*

1992

The Chicago Architecture
Award
Illinois Council/AIA

1991

Award of Excellence
AIA/The American Library
Association
*Las Vegas Library and
Children's Museum*

Honor Award
AIA/Los Angeles Chapter
Design Awards Program
*Mandell Weiss Forum
and La Jolla Playhouse*

Architectural Digest
100 Architects

Honor Award
California Council AIA
Venice House

Nissan International Fellow
Aspen Design Conference

Zimmerman Award
University of New Mexico,
Albuquerque

1990

Merit Award
AIA/Los Angeles Chapter
Design Awards Program
Venice House

Best in Institutional Design
Twelfth Annual Interior
Awards, *Interiors Magazine*
*Las Vegas Library
and Children's Museum*

AIA National Honor Award
Nelson Fine Arts Center

Citation
Progressive Architecture
Annual Awards Program
*American Heritage Center
and Art Museum*

Award of
Excellence for Design
*Architectural Record:
Record Houses
Zuber House*

Firm Award
Western Mountain Region
AIA

Citation
Western Mountain Region
AIA
Venice House

Award for Excellence
in Architecture
Western Mountain Region
AIA
Zuber House

Award for Excellence
in Architecture
Western Mountain Region
AIA
*Las Vegas Library and
Children's Museum*

1989

Gran Premio
Internacional de la
Bienal Internacional
de Arquitectura
de Buenos Aires
Nelson Fine Arts Center

Award for
Excellence in Architecture
Western Mountain Region
AIA
Nelson Fine Arts Center

Distinguished
Alumni Award
University of New Mexico,
Albuquerque

220

The lobby intentionally creates ambiguity: is the visitor/spectator part of the realm of theater, or simply a presence in the lobby? The building from above

1987

AIA National Honor Award
Fuller House

Award for
Excellence in Architecture
Western Mountain Region
AIA
Troy House

Award for
Excellence in Architecture
Western Mountain Region
AIA
Lazarus House

Award for
Excellence in Architecture
Western Mountain Region
AIA
New Mexico Heart Clinic

1986

Award of
Excellence for Design
Architectural Record:
Record Houses
Rio Grande Valley House

Honor Award
Western Mountain Region
AIA
Fuller House

Honor Award
Western Mountain Region
AIA
The Beach Apartments

Honor Award
Western Mountain Region
AIA
Rio Grande Valley House

1985–1986

Merit Award
AIA and *Sunset Magazine*:
Western Home Awards
Rio Grande Valley House

1985

Citation
Progressive Architecture
Annual Awards Program
The Beach Apartments

Rome Prize Fellow
American Academy
in Rome

1984

Citation
Progressive Architecture
Annual Awards Program
Desert Highlands

Honor Award
Western Mountain Region
AIA
Rio Grande Nature Center

1983

Honor Award
Western Mountain Region
AIA
United Blood Services

1982

Award of
Excellence for Design
Architectural Record:
Record Houses
Santa Fe House

1981–1982

Citation
AIA and *Sunset Magazine*:
Western Home Awards
Tennis Ranch of Taos

1981

AIA Fellow

1978

Merit Award
Western Mountain Region
AIA
Chant House

1977

Award of
Excellence for Design
Architectural Record:
Record Houses
Mountain House

1973

Merit Award
Western Mountain Region
AIA
First National Bank,
Sandia Plaza

1971

Merit Award
Western Mountain Region
AIA
Predock House and Studio

1970

Award of
Excellence for Design
Architectural Record:
Record Houses
La Luz Community

1969–1970

Citation
AIA and *Sunset Magazine*:
Western Home Awards
Raven Townhouse

1962–1963

William Kinne Fellows
Memorial Traveling
Fellowship
Columbia University

221

...itar; its scale responds to the high-speed "audience" on University Boulevard as well as to the campus pedestrian.

INVITED COMPETITIONS

1993

Winner

*Center for Integrated
Systems Expansion*

Stanford University

Palo Alto, California

1992

Finalist

*Clark County
Government Center*

Las Vegas, Nevada

1991

Finalist

*Texas Rangers
Baseball Park*

Arlington, Texas

Finalist

*South Transept,
St. John The Divine*

New York, New York

1994

Finalist

*Baltimore Performing
Arts Center*

Baltimore, Maryland

Finalist

*Maryland Center
for Performing Arts*

College Park, Maryland

Finalist

Atlantis Hotel and Casino

ITT Sheraton

Las Vegas, Nevada

1990

Finalist

Agadir Palm Bay Resort

Agadir, Morocco

1989

Winner

*United States Pavilion
World Expo '92*

Seville, Spain

(Alternate design
constructed.)

1987

Winner

CLA Cal Poly

California Polytechnic State
University at Pomona

1986

Finalist

Charleston Aquarium

Charleston, South Carolina

Winner

*American Heritage Center
and Art Museum*

University of Wyoming
at Laramie

Winner

*Las Vegas Library and
Children's Museum*

Las Vegas, Nevada

1985

Winner

Nelson Fine Arts Center

Arizona State University

Tempe, Arizona

SELECTED EXHIBITIONS

1993

Antoine Predock
University of Wyoming
Art Museum, Laramie

"Angel Art"
Pacific Design Center,
Los Angeles, California

"AIA Art By Architects"
Exhibition/Auction
Chicago, Illinois

Antoine Predock
CAFE Gallery,
Albuquerque, New Mexico

1992

"Contemporary
Architectural Drawing"
GA Gallery, Tokyo, Japan

"The Architect's Sketchbook:
Current Practice"
Canadian Center
for Architecture,
Montreal, Canada

Six New Mexico Houses"
University Art Museum,
University of New Mexico,
Albuquerque

1991

"St. John the Divine
South Transept"
Urban Center,
New York, New York

"Third Belgrade Triennial
of World Architecture"
Belgrade, Yugoslavia

"Seville World Expo '92"
University of California
at Los Angeles
School of Architecture

1990

"Architects/Designers/
Planners for a Socially
Responsible Environment
USA/USSR Exhibit"
New York City; Moscow;
Tempe, Arizona

"Architects & Sketchbooks"
Getty Center, Los Angeles,
California

"Living Space: Contemporary
Western Architecture"
Contemporary Art Museum,
Colorado Springs

1989

"Nelson Fine Arts Center"
Bienal '89 Arquitectura,
Buenos Aires, Argentina

"Playspaces"
Des Moines Art Center,
Iowa

1988

"Antoine Predock, Architect:
Landscape Apparitions"
John Nichols Gallery,
New York, New York

"California Lifeguard
Towers"
Kirsten Kiser Gallery,
Los Angeles, California

"Unbuilt Architecture
of the 80s"
Cooper-Hewitt Museum,
New York, New York

"Harvard Graduate
Design Studio"
Student Work and
Las Vegas Project Model
Las Vegas, Nevada

"Architects/Designers/
Planners for Social
Responsibility:
Fourth Benefit Auction and
International Exhibition
of Architectural Drawings"
Max Protetch Gallery,
New York, New York

1987

"Antoine Predock:
Recent Works"
Harvard University
Graduate School of Design,
Cambridge, Massachusetts

"The Inhabited Landscape"
Urban Center,
New York, New York

"Antoine Predock:
Frammenti d'Italia"
Graham Gallery,
Albuquerque, New Mexico

1985

"Annual Exhibition"
American Academy in Rome

1984

"Times Tower Competition"
Urban Center,
New York, New York

1981

"Des Architectures de Terre"
Centre Georges Pompidou,
Paris

"The Making of an Architect"
National Academy of Design,
New York, New York

223

1994

Anderson, Kurt. "Architecture: Antoine Predock, Serious Modernism in Dallas," *Architectural Digest*, March 1994, 104–11
Turtle Creek House.

Dillon, David. "Making Ripples on the Range," *The Dallas Morning News*, March 6, 1994
American Heritage Center and Art Museum.

Fraser, Iain and Rod Henmi. *Envisioning Architecture: An Analysis of Drawing*, New York: Van Nostrand Reinhold, 1994, 84–85, 125–29.

GA Houses 42. Tokyo: A.D.A. EDITA Tokyo Co., July 1994, 68–93
House.

Gubitosi, Alessandro. "The Elemental Spirit," *L'Arca*, May 1994, 46–53

Pearson, Clifford A. "For the Birds," *Architectural Record: Record Houses*, April 1994, 76–83
Turtle Creek House.

Top 10 Best Design of 1993," *Time*, January 3, 1994, 72
Turtle Creek House.

1993

Betsky, Aaron. "Magic Marker," *Architectural Record*, February 1993, 62–69
CLA Cal Poly.

———. "World in Motion: Architect Antoine Predock Choreographs L.A.," *LA Weekly*, June 18–24, 1993, 30–31.

"'Desire Lines' Cast in Stone," *Architectural Record*, April 1993, 25
Bookstore and Parking Structure.

GA Houses 37. Tokyo: A.D.A. EDITA Tokyo Co., March 1993, 114–15
House.

Giovannini, Joseph. "Vorgeschichtlicher Vulkan," *Frankfurter Allgemeine*, December 3, 1993
American Heritage Center and Art Museum.

———. "Western Frontiers: Myth and Spirit," *Architecture*, December 1993, 47–61
American Heritage Center and Art Museum.

Jodidio, Philip. *Contemporary American Architects.* Germany: Benedikt Taschen, 1993, 141–51
Hotel Santa Fe, Zuber House, Nelson Fine Arts Center, Las Vegas Library and Children's Museum.

Webb, Michael. "Mandell Weiss Forum," *A + U*, January 1993, 30–45
Mandell Weiss Forum and La Jolla Playhouse.

1992

Allégret, Laurence. *Musées 2* Paris: Editions du Moniteur, 1992, 113
Nelson Fine Arts Center.

The American House: Design For Living . Washington D.C. and Australia: AIA Press and The Images Publishing Group, 1992, 44–45
Venice House.

The Architect's Sketchbook: Current Practice Exhibition catalog, Montreal: Canadian Centre for Architecture, 1992, 16–17.

Collyer, Stanley. "Antoine Predock," *Competitions* (Winter 1992), 50–61.

Dietsch, Deborah K. "Desert Trails," *Architecture*, July 1992, 48–51
Hotel Santa Fe.

———. "Shame in Spain," *Architecture*, April 1992, 15
United States Pavilion.

Gustmann, Kurt. "Antoine Predock: Die Groben Architekten" *Hauser*, April 1992, 59–70.

Horn, Miriam. "The Rise of the Desert Rat," *Vanity Fair*, March 1992, 112–22.

"Hotel Santa Fe," *Connaissance des Arts* (April 1992), 46–51
Hotel Santa Fe.

Hotel Specification International England: Pennington Press Limited, 1992, 16–17
Hotel Santa Fe.

Hume, Christopher. "Predock Drags Design Back Into The Real World," *The Toronto Star*, November 14, 1992, F10
Nelson Fine Arts Center.

Kahn, Eve M. "Antoine Predock on Campus," *The Wall Street Journal*, October 23, 1992, A12
CLA Cal Poly.

Koerble, Barbara L. "Texas Rangers Ballpark Competition," *A + U*, April 1992, 3–5
Texas Rangers Baseball Park.

McGuigan, Cathleen. "Apres Mickey, le Deluge," *Newsweek*, April 13, 1992, 16–18
Hotel Santa Fe.

Moiraghi, Luigi. "The Ship of the Desert," *L'Arca*, July–August 1992, 12–15
Ship of the Desert.

Morris, Roger. "New Star in Santa Fe," *Architectural Digest*, June 1992, 82–88
Institute of American Indian Arts Museum.

"The New Nature of Architecture," *Metropolis*, April 1992, 45
Nelson Fine Arts Center; Las Vegas Library and Children's Museum; South Transept, St. John the Divine

"Predock Science Museum Rises in Arizona Desert," *Architectural Record*, May 1992, 22
Arizona Museum of Science.

Price, V. B. *A City at the End of the World* Albuquerque: V. B. Price, 1992, 33–35, 75, 78, 85, 92–93
The Beach Apartments, La Luz Community, Albuquerque Museum.

Rockwell, John. "At Euro-Disney Hotels, Another Fantasyland," *The New York Times*, April 14, 1992, B1
Hotel Santa Fe.

Rybczynski, Witold. "A Good Public Building," *The Atlantic*, August 1992, 84–87
Las Vegas Library and Children's Museum.

"Six International Architects Discuss Their Design Approaches to Integrating Houses into the Natural Environment," *Architectural Digest*, September 1992, 48
Ship of the Desert, Troy House.

Webb, Michael. "Architecture: Antoine Predock, Desert Forms Define an Arizona Residence," *Architectural Digest*, March 1992, 142–49, 194
Winandy House.

1991–1992

Mulard, Claudine. "Las Vegas: Musee des enfants," *Architecture Interieure Crée*, December 1991–January 1992, 130–33
Las Vegas Library and Children's Museum.

1991

Architectural Digest: The AD 100 Architects. New York: Architectural Digest Publishing Corp., 1991, 188–89
Troy House, Venice House, Tesuque House.

Architectural Houses 5: Houses by the Sea. Barcelona: Ediciones Atrium, 1991, 228–36
Venice House.

Boissiere, Olivier. "Antoine Predock: Architect of the West," *Vogue Decoration*, February–March 1991, 53–61.

Dibar, Carlos, and Diego Armando. "Antoine Predock: Filtrando imagenes," *Arquitectura e Urbanismo*, February–March 1991, 36–49
Nelson Fine Arts Center, Venice House, Fuller House, American Heritage Center and Art Museum.

Dixon, John Morris. "Transcendence on the Beach," *Progressive Architecture*, April 1991, 92–95
Venice House.

GA Document 30. Tokyo: A.D.A. EDITA Tokyo Co., August 1991, 108–17
Las Vegas Library and Children's Museum.

GA Houses 31. Tokyo: A.D.A. EDITA Tokyo Co., March 1991, 59–61
Rosenthal House.

GA Houses 32. Tokyo: A.D.A. EDITA Tokyo Co., July 1991, 116–25
Zuber House.

Garrison, Renee. "New Magic for MOSI," *Tampa Tribune*, March 1, 1991
Tampa Museum of Science and Industry.

Giordano, Michele Bazan, "La Cittadella dell'arte," *L'Arca*, March 1991, 10–21.
Nelson Fine Arts Center.

Horn, Miriam. "Designing in Hues of Green," *U.S. News & World Report*, February 25, 1991, 58–59
La Luz Community.

———. "A Master of Contradictions," *Graphis*, November–December 1991, 81–87.

Jencks, Charles. *The Language of Post-Modern Architecture, The Sixth Edition.* New York: Rizzoli International Publications, 1991, 192–95
Nelson Fine Arts Center.

Johnson, Jory, and Felice Frankel. *Modern Landscape Architecture: Redefining the Garden.* New York: Abbeville Press, 1991, 131–41
Fuller House.

"Keil dur die City," *Stern*, July 4, 1991, 40–52
Nelson Fine Arts Center.

Lacy, Bill. *100 Contemporary Architects.* New York: Harry N. Abrams, Inc., 1991, Pages 186–87
Nelson Fine Arts Center.

Mitchell, Shane. "Desert Mania," *Interiors*, January 1991, 110–11
Las Vegas Library and Children's Museum.

"New Civic Center for Thousand Oaks," *Architectural Record*, July 1991, 66
Thousand Oaks Civic Arts Plaza.

Posner, Ellen. "Supporting Role," *Architecture*, September 1991, 47–53
Mandell Weiss Forum and La Jolla Playhouse.

St. John, David, and Antoine Predock. *Terraces of Rain: An Italian Sketchbook.* Santa Fe: Recursos Press, 1991
Drawings.

Sainz, Jorge. "Con el mar en el salon, casa en la playa, Venice," *A&V* (Monographias de Arquitectura & Vivienda), November–December 1991, 38–41
Venice House.

1990

"American Heritage Center and Art Museum," *Progressive Architecture*, January 1990, 96–98.
American Heritage Center and Art Museum.

"The Best of America," *U.S. News & World Report*, July 9, 1990, 61
Nelson Fine Arts Center.

Boissiere, Olivier. "Antoine Predock," *L'Architecture d'Aujourd'hui*, October 1990, 177–87.

Cecchetti, Maurizio. "Un Centro per la memoria collettiva," *L'Arca*, October 1990, 40–47
American Heritage Center and Art Museum.

Cheek, Lawrence W. "Desert Blooms," *Architecture*, January 1990, 92–97
Nelson Fine Arts Center.

GA Houses 28. Tokyo: A.D.A. EDITA Tokyo Co., March 1990, 67–69
Turtle Creek House, Winandy House.

GA Houses 30. Tokyo: A.D.A. EDITA Tokyo Co., December 1990, 118–21
Venice House.

Goldberger, Paul. "Drawing the Past is Like Describing an Elephant," *New York Times*, October 7, 1990.

———. "Speaking the Language of Desert and Mountain," *The New York Times*, January 28, 1990, 37–38
Nelson Fine Arts Center.

Lavin, Sylvia. "El Desierto edificado: Predock, centro de arte en Arizona," *Arquitectura Viva*, November–December 1990, 24–28
Nelson Fine Arts Center.

———. "Dynamics of Venice Beach," *Architectural Digest*, December 1990, 120–23, 218
Venice House.

———. "Power to Heal," *Elle Decor*, June–July 1990, 80–88
Nelson Fine Arts Center, Zuber House.

"Magic and Power in the Landscape," *Landscape Architecture*, June 1990, 56–59
Hotel Santa Fe.

Hispanic Cultural Center   Albuquerque, New Mexico

This project diagrams cultural patterns and connections. For instance, the paseo, *the evening walk, is a critical*

Posner, Ellen. "Building with Desert, Mountains and Light," *Wall Street Journal*, March 6, 1990, A16
Nelson Fine Arts Center.

————. "Media and Architecture," *Quaderns* 184 (1990), 24–29.

————. "We Are In The Desert," *Landscape Architecture*, August 1990, 42–45
American Heritage Center and Art Museum, Nelson Fine Arts Center, The Beach Apartments, Rio Grande Nature Center, Fuller House.

Stein, Karen D. "Down the Strip," *Architectural Record*, October 1990, 68–75
Las Vegas Library and Children's Museum.

————. "Raising Arizona,"
Architectural Record: Record Houses, Mid-April 1990, 88–95
Zuber House.

Tonka, Hubert. *Architecture & Cie. 2*. Paris: Les Editions du Demi-Cercle, 1990, 57–72
Nelson Fine Arts Center and Art Museum.

Wright, Gwendolyn, and Janet Parks, eds. *The History of History in American Schools of Architecture 1865–1975*. New York: The Temple Hoyne Buell Center for the Study of American Architecture and Princeton Architectural Press, 1990, 182
Drawings.

1989–1990
Loriers, Marie-Christine, "Monts Et Merveilles," *Techniques & Architecture*, December 1989–January 1990, 90–95
Nelson Fine Arts Center.

Mulard, Claudine. "Antoine Predock," *Architecture Interieure Crée*, December 1989–January 1990.

1989
"Antoine Predock: Un caso d'inclusività sintetica'," *L'Architettura*, March 1989, 178–98.

Boles, Daralice D. "Magic Mountain," *Progressive Architecture*, June 1989, 65–77
Nelson Fine Arts Center.

Farnsworth, Christina. "A 'Dream Mystic' Makes His Mark on Architecture," *Professional Builder*, Mid-October 1989, 17–22
Venice House, Fuller House.

GA Document 24. Tokyo: A.D.A. EDITA Tokyo Co., August 1989, 6–19
Nelson Fine Arts Center.

Moiraghi, Luigi. "Un Nuovo segno per Las Vegas," *L'Arca*, September 1989, 52–59
Las Vegas Library and Children's Museum.

Playspaces: Architecture for Children. Exhibition catalog, Des Moines, Iowa: Des Moines Art Center, 1989, 41–47
Spectral Slug, Fuller House.

Plummer, Henry. *The Potential House: Three Centuries of American Dwelling*. Tokyo: *A + U* Publishing Co., September 1989, 244–57
Fuller House.

Sacchi, Livio. *Il Disegno dell'architettura Americana*. Rome: Guis. Editori Laterza, 1989, 274–77
Rio Grande Valley House, Fuller House, Tesuque House, The Beach Apartments, Desert Highlands.

1988
Anderson, Kurt. "An Architect for the New Age," *Time*, April 11, 1988, 72.

"Antoine Predock," *A + U*, November 1988, 75–130.

Campbell, Robert. "Antoine Predock: Redefining the Traditional Hacienda Near Santa Fe," *Architectural Digest*, April 1988, 18–23
Lazarus House.

Dillon, David. "Regionalism, But With Many Inventive Twists," *Architecture*, July 1988, 84–87
Lazarus House.

Haber, Francine. *Contemporary Architecture 10*. Paris: Bibliothéque des Arts, 1988, 45–48
Rio Grande Nature Center, La Luz Community, United Blood Services, The Beach Apartments, Lazarus House.

Lemos, Paul. "Antoine's Altered States," *London Sunday Times Magazine*, June 19, 1988, 76–77
Fuller House, United Blood Services, CLA Cal Poly.

Predock, Antoine. *Studio Work, Harvard University Graduate School of Design, 1987–88*. Cambridge: Harvard University Graduate School of Design, 1988, 38.

————. "Unity and Diversity,"
L'Arca, June 1988, 52–57
CLA Cal Poly.

Price, V. B. "Antoine Predock, FAIA," *Artspace*, Winter 1987–88, 70–78

Stein, Karen D. "Five Projects: Antoine Predock, Architect," *Architectural Record*, October 1988, 88–97
Housing, Retail, Auditorium; American Heritage Center and Art Museum; Nelson Fine Arts Center; CLA Cal Poly; Mandell Weiss Forum and La Jolla Playhouse.

1987
Freeman, Allen. "Forms As Rugged As Their Desert Setting," *Architecture*, May 1987, 128–13?
Fuller House.

GA Houses 21. Tokyo: A.D.A. EDITA Tokyo Co., February 1987, 74–115.

GA Houses Special 2: The Emerging Generation in U.S.A. Tokyo: A.D.A. EDITA Tokyo Co., November 1987, 52–55
Zuber House.

Hispanic Cultural Center

element in Spanish culture, and this project provides many opportunities to walk: under sheltered arcades, across plazas, and through courtyards. The

Geibel, Victoria. "The Allure of Water," *Metropolis*, July–August 1987, 39–45
Rio Grande Nature Center.

The Inhabited Landscape. Exhibition catalog. New York: The Architectural League of New York, 1987
Fuller House.

Morris, Roger. "Architecture: Antoine Predock," *Architectural Digest*, August 1987, 90–97, 115
Troy House.

Places, 4, no. 4. Cambridge: The MIT Press, 1987, 24–25
Rio Grande Nature Center.

1986

Adams, Robert M. "Desert Spirit," *House & Garden*, December 1986, 132–41, 202–4
Fuller House.

Anderson, Grace. "Landscape Memories," *Architectural Record: Record Houses*, Mid-April 1986, 72–79
Rio Grande Valley House.

Canty, Donald. "Colorful Regional 'Landscape' Celebrates Route 66," *Architecture*, October 1986, 78–81
The Beach Apartments.

Crosbie, Michael. "'Vibrant' Italian Sketches," *Architecture*, January 1986, Page 23.

Goldberger, Paul. "Architecture: Antoine Predock," *Architectural Digest*, October 1986, 178–83
Tesuque House.

1985

"The Beach," *Progressive Architecture*, January 1985, Pages 108–9
The Beach Apartments.

Predock, Antoine. *Italian Sketchbooks.* Rome: Antoine Predock, 1985.

1984

Crosbie, Michael J. "Kaleidoscope: Nature Center Stands in the Water Like a Sculpted Dam," *Architecture*, December 1984, 72–73
Rio Grande Nature Center.

"Desert Highlands," *Progressive Architecture*, January 1984, 126–28
Desert Highlands.

"Edelstein mit neuem Schliff," *Hauser*, April 1984, 116–23.

"La Luz-Stadt in der Sonne," *Hauser*, March 1984, 254–61
La Luz Community.

Papademetriou, Peter C. "Blind Trust," *Progressive Architecture*, March 1984, 86–90
Rio Grande Nature Center.

Triglyph. Tempe: College of Architecture and Environmental Design, Arizona State University, Fall 1984, 24–27
Desert Highlands.

1981

Des Architectures De Terre. Paris: Centre Georges Pompidou/CCI, 1981, 146–47, 178–81.
La Luz Community.

Kidder-Smith, G. E., with The Museum of Modern Art, New York. *The Architecture of the United States, Volume 3.* New York: Anchor Press/Doubleday, 1981, 512–13
La Luz Community.

1980

"Post-Modernists: Out of the Glass Box," *Forbes Magazine* (Arabic Annual Issue), 1980, 29–31
La Luz Community.

1979

Decorative Art and Modern Interiors: Themes in Nature. New York: William Morrow and Company, Inc., 1979, 66–73
Mountain House.

1978

Modern Houses in America. Tokyo: Process Architecture Publishing Co., 1978, 164–67
Mountain House.

1977

Gordon, Barclay F. "Record Houses of 1977," *Architectural Record: Record Houses*, May 1977, 60–61
Mountain House.

A View of Contemporary World Architects. Japan: Shinkenchiku-Sha, 1977, 260.

1976

Hoyt, Charles K. "Even Small Banks Can Express A Regional Vernacular," *Architectural Record*, September 1976, Pages 124–26
First National Bank: Sandia Plaza Branch

1974

"Kaminsky House," *A + U*, June 1974, 14–15
Kaminsky House.

"Regionalism: The Southwest," *Progressive Architecture*, March 1974, 60–69.
La Luz Community, The Citadel Apartments, Kaminsky House, First National Bank: Sandia Plaza.

1971

Davidson, Marshall B. *American Heritage History of Notable American Houses.* New York: American Heritage Publishing Co., Inc., 1971, 352–53
La Luz Community.

Predock, Antoine. "La Luz, Albuquerque, N.M.," *Architecture d'Aujourd'hui*, September 1971, 70–73
La Luz Community.

1970

Macasi, John. *Housing.* New York: John Wiley & Sons, Inc., 1976, 445
The Citadel Apartments.

1969

"La Luz," *Architectural Forum*, July 1969, 65–70
La Luz Community.

rds are sites for various performances and gatherings. Gardens are intermingled with the courtyards: functional gardens, milpitas, in which remedios (herbs) can be

PHOTO CREDITS

Peter Aaron / Esto
Hotel Santa Fe
Pages 164,
165 lower, 166,
168 upper left, 169 lower,
171, 172 lower, 174

Tom Bonner
Thousand Oaks
Civic Arts Plaza
Page 162

Solana Office Building
Page 219

Mary Elkins
Hotel Santa Fe
Page 172 upper

Baltimore Performing
Arts Center
All photos

Mediterranean Hotel
Page 102

School of Music
University of California
at Santa Cruz
Page 218

Butterfly Garden
Page 219

Scott Frances / Esto
Hotel Santa Fe
Pages 168 right, 173 lower

Douglas L. Friend
Rosenthal House
All photos

Joshua Freiwald
La Luz Community
Pages 22, 27

Kaminsky House
Page 216

Mountain House
Page 216

First National Bank:
Sandia Plaza
Page 216

Jerry Goffe
La Luz Community
Title page,
Pages 20, 24, 29, 32

Tim Griffith
CLA Cal Poly
Page 162
The Images Publishing
Group, Ltd.

David Hewitt /Anne Garrison
Mandell Weiss Forum
and La Jolla Playhouse
Page 141

Timothy Hurlsey
Rio Grande Nature Center
All photos except
pages 19 upper right,
25 upper left and
upper right, 26

Fuller House
All photos

Nelson Fine Arts Center
All photos except
page 79

Zuber House
All photos except
pages 80, 90

Las Vegas Library
and Children's Museum
All photos except
pages 98, 100 upper left,
111, 115

Venice House
All photos except
pages 116, 128, 129

Mandell Weiss Forum
and La Jolla Playhouse
All photos except
pages 130, 141, 147

CLA Cal Poly
All photos except
page 162

Turtle Creek House
Pages 181 upper right,
182, 186, 187, 188,
190, 191 lower right, 193,
195 upper right,
196 upper left

American Heritage Center
and Art Museum
All photos

Rio Grande Valley House
Page 217

Mary Nichols
Venice House
Pages 116, 128, 129
courtesy of
Architectural Digest
© 1990 The Conde Nast
Publications.
All rights reserved.
Used with permission.

228

grown, and formal gardens. Accomodating cultural ceremonies, principally those centered around food, was an important part of the program, and the kitch

229

the ampitheater and informal dining areas and can serve as a sidewalk café, was designed as a demonstration kitchen. Subtle processions through the project

STUDIO

Staff (1967—94)

Geoffrey Adams
D. Joseph Andrade
A. Anthony Anella

Matthew Baird	Phyllis Cece
Sunil R. Bald	Margaret Chambers
Nanci Baldwin	Sandra L. Cheromiah
Victoria Baran	Ned Cherry
Joseph K. Barden, Jr.	Michael T. Chin
John W. Bass	Linda M. Christensen
Donald C. Bennett	Terrance Cisco
Marcus A. Blasi	Arthur Thomas Corsie
Lawrence B. Blough	Shawn J. Delisio
Kathleen M. Bost	Mark T. DePree
Stephen C. Boston	Eileen Devereux
Gail Boyer	Angela E. Dirks
John C. Brittingham	Dan Dixson
Ann Bromberg	Betty Marie Duffy
Mark L. Bruzan	Ronald J. Duhamel
Luke Bulman	Edward Eeds
Jorge R. Burbano	Raouf El-Beleidy
Patty Burling	Cameron C. Erdmann
Christopher L. Calott	Juan P. Fabres
Kathleen Campbell	Beth Ann Farley
Leslie A. Campbell	Glen Fellows
Judith L. Carroll	Madonna Fernando
Michele Marie Caruthers	Derek S. Fisher

Current Staff

Deanna Lynn Chino
Devendra Contractor
Mark K. Donahue
Mischa L. Farrell
Paul L. Gonzales
Thea Hahn
Regina Lynn Harris
Robert F. McElheney
R. Lawrence Mead
George Newlands
Darrell Brett Oaks
Kira A. Sowanick

Former Associates

Jon R. Anderson
Van H. Gilbert
Ronald J. Jacob
Lawrence Licht
Stanley G. Moore
A. S. Predock
Glade Sperry, Jr.

Associates

Geoffrey A. Beebe
W. Anthony Evanko
Douglas L. Friend

230 Derek Thomas Payne

Hispanic Cultural Center

come together, culminating in a new vantage point atop a torreon, looking out across the valley. This building quietly alludes to Mesoamerican forms.

John D. Fleming
Ira Frazin
Jon Van Gaasbeek
Allene Gibson
Pankaj Gupta
Lorraine Guthrie
Gabriella Frances Gutierrez
Reginalda Gutierrez
Pamela Harling
Sanna M. Harma
Robert Mark Harris
I. Craig Holdren
James R. Horn
Katharine E. Howe
David A. Hrabal
C. Aron Idoine
Rebecca A. Ingram

Jennifer Jardine
James C. Johnson
Janet R. Johnston
Peter F. Karsten
Jocelyn F. Kasero
Kevin Kellogg
Jane Frances King
Karen Jean King
William Konopik
Pamela Ku
Peter J. Lagomarsino
Mark B. Lawton
Matthew R. Lawton
Karen T. Lente
Scott Alan Lindenau
Jennifer Predock-Linnell
Armando Lopez
Jose G. Lopez
Gregory S. Lynn
Daniel G. Macias
Pedro A. Marquez
Steven R. Maurice
Cara McCulloch-Lieuwen
Ann McLaughlin
Romeo Medina, Jr.
C. Courtney Mercer
Kim Miller
David P. Mishler
Edward George Mitchell
Snow Moore
Marcia Morris
Catherine Mullinax-Jones

Nancy E. Napheys
David A. Nelson
Elizabeth Nicewander
Timothy W. Nichols
Gary Nolen
Luella Noles
Norman Noonan

Thomas R. Ortiz
Kelton E. Osborn
Steven M. Osborn
Thomas William Parks
Jennifer Pepe
Lawrence Pevec
Dorothy J. Pierson
Jean L. Pike
Todd Pilgreen
Hadrian Predock
Jason Predock
Thomas A. Piekenbrock
Denise E. Purley
A. Christopher Purvis
Rebecca L. Quigley
Larry Railey
Ruben Miguel Ramirez

David Reddy
Ginny Reid
Rebecca J. Riden
Richard E. Rivera
Keith D. Robertson
Dennis Rodriguez
Timothy J. Rohleder
Christopher T. Romero
Rob P. Romero
Rachel Leah Rosenthal
Margaret Ross
Steve Routen
Sunil S. Sakhalkar
Kenneth Sandoval
Alcides Santiesteban
Curtis J. Scharfenaker
James See
Ronald Shafer
Lisa G. Sharp
Kimberly J. Smith
Richard V. Smith
David M. Somoza
Kevin D. Spence
Catherine Spencer
Joanne Spencer
Christopher M. Stachecki
Samuel M. Sterling

Douglas W. Strech
John Scott Taylor
John C. Toomey
Hajime J. Uesato
Donald H. Vanderpool
Stephanie A. Vencil
James W. Visscher
Deborah Waldrip
E. Suzanne Weisman
Michael E. Wewerka
James I. Williams II
Jeffrey Winter
David Witherspoon
Kramer E. Woodard
Jeffrey S. Wren
Alexia A. Zerbinis